The Last Trumpet

The Mystery of God is Finished and a New Age Begins

R O B E R T
J O H N S T O N

WinePressPublishing
Great Books, Defined.

WinePressPublishing
Great Books, Defined.

To order additional copies of this book call:
1-877-421-READ (7323)
or please visit our website at
www.WinePressbooks.com

If you enjoyed this quality custom-published book,
drop by our website for more books and information.
www.winepresspublishing.com
"Your partner in custom publishing."

ISBN 13: 978-1-60615-071-9
ISBN 10: 1-60615-071-5
Library of Congress Catalog Card Number: 2010934100

To the Jewish people, who have suffered long, and to their land, which has been a stumbling block for the nations. I thank you for the wonderful heritage you have given to the world and for the place you have in God's heart. I look forward to the day when you will be called Hephzibah (My Delight) and your land Beulah (Married).

To my faithful brothers in Christ and faithful servants of Christ, who have supported me and been a sounding board for me. I am forever grateful to John Domino, Bill Brower, Doug Mills, and Barry Maney.

To my wonderful wife, who shares the love of the truth with me, encourages me to write the truth, and questions me about things that are hard to understand.

Contents

The secret things belong unto the Lord our God: but the things which are revealed belong unto us, and to our children for ever, that we may do all the words of this law.

—Deuteronomy 29:29

Introduction

*And I saw the seven angels which stood before God; and to them
were given seven trumpets.*

—Revelation 8:2

WHEN THE LAST seal is opened in heaven, seven angels with
seven trumpets will announce the final events that will end this
present age. The seventh and last trumpet, however, will not only
conclude this present age but also announce the beginning of a
new age on this restored earth, where righteousness will reign
for a thousand years. This day of transition is known as the day
of the Lord.

The day of the Lord is the fulfillment of a prophecy and a
promise God gave when Paradise was lost that Jesus would one
day return to earth to live with mankind. This expectation, the
great hope of mankind since the beginning, was passed down
from generation to generation, survived the great flood of Noah's
day, and continues to this present generation. God made the
promise on the day sin and death entered the world after Satan's
temptation and Adam's fall.

The hope of the Lord's return will be fulfilled on the day when
the promise, the Messiah, the seed of the woman, will crush
Antichrist, the seed of Satan. The promise, passed down from
Adam and Eve through their son Seth and his generations, is the

hope for all who believe. For the unrighteous or the unbelieving, however, the day of the Lord will be a day of destruction similar to the destruction of mankind in Noah's flood, except this time the destruction will not come by flood.

The generations of Adam and Eve's firstborn son, Cain, continued to live in rebellion against God, and the world became so wicked in Noah's day that God judged it to be "depraved and putrid" (Gen. 6:11 AMP). Therefore, he destroyed mankind off the face of the earth. The Bible tells us that "as were the days of Noah, so will be the coming of the Son of Man" (Matt. 24:37 AMP).

PROMISES

After the flood God called a man named Abraham and promised to bring him and his descendants to a land called Canaan (present-day Israel), where the land would become an everlasting possession for them. The vision God gave to Abraham was more than just a vision of the land. Abraham saw beyond the day of the Lord in a distant vision of heaven, similar to that shown to the apostle John, of a new heaven and a new earth and a "new Jerusalem" coming down from heaven, bedecked with precious stones (Rev. 21:2, 10–11). He also beheld the glory of God dwelling with man forever (v. 3). Although Abraham never experienced the fulfillment of the vision's promise during his lifetime, the vision guided his journey on earth. Hebrews 11:10 says, "For he was looking for the city which has foundations, whose architect and builder is God" (NASB). (See Rev. 21:14, 19–20 for Abraham's vision of the foundations.)

Abraham wasn't the only one who didn't see the promises fulfilled in his lifetime. The great chapter of faith in the book of Hebrews describes several men and women of faith who also wanted to see the eternal city, the New Jerusalem. Mentioned in this chapter are Abel, Enoch, Noah, Sarah, Isaac, and Joseph.

> All these died in faith, without receiving the promises, but having seen them and having welcomed them from a distance, and having confessed that they were strangers and exiles on the earth. For those who say such things make it clear that they are seeking a country of their own. . . . But as it is, they desire a better country, that is, a heavenly one. Therefore God is not ashamed to be called their God; for He has prepared a city for them.
>
> —Hebrews 11:13–14, 16 (NASB)

A righteous man named Job lived during the same period as Abraham. In his darkest hour, when he was convinced that he was about to die, Job testified about his greatest hope, the day of the Lord, when he would be resurrected to life. "And as for me, I know that my Redeemer lives, and at the last He will take His stand on the earth. Even after my skin is destroyed, yet from my flesh I shall see God; whom I myself shall behold, and whom my eyes will see and not another" (Job 19:25–27 NASB).

In the wilderness God gave Moses a pattern (Ex. 25:9) for the future temple of the Lord, which he wanted built in Jerusalem. He also gave instructions in Leviticus 23:39–42 for the tabernacles (booths) that would be used during the Feast of Tabernacles, which the Jews and all nations would celebrate annually even following the day of the Lord. The Old Testament prophets also gave many prophecies about the day of the Lord to the nation of Israel. These can be found in Isaiah 2:2; Daniel 7:14; Joel 2:11; Micah 4:1; and Malachi 4:1, among others.

The day of the Lord is a special day God first promised in Genesis 3:15 to Adam and Eve on the day they lost eternal life. In this book we will examine specific events, starting with Christ's last days before his death and resurrection. Then we will look at the advent of his return for his people, including the resurrection and rapture of the saints. We will learn about the defeat of Antichrist, the binding of Satan, and the beginning of God's kingdom on earth. Appropriately, we will conclude with a description of our final destination—heaven.

This book is written primarily from the words of Jesus and his apostles. These words and promises blend perfectly with the many prophecies and promises God made to those in the Old Testament and directed to the nation of Israel. It has been written with the knowledge and understanding that Gentile (non-Jewish) believers will stand with God's chosen people, the Jews, and that we will all stand in our place on the day of the Lord.

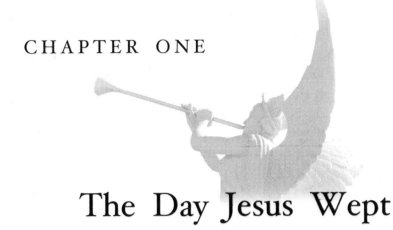

CHAPTER ONE

The Day Jesus Wept

O Jerusalem, Jerusalem, thou that killest the prophets, and stonest them which are sent unto thee, how often would I have gathered thy children together, even as a hen gathereth her chickens under her wings, and ye would not!

—Matthew 23:37

THE WEEK WHEN Jesus was crucified is perhaps the most meaningful time in history to understand God's plan for the ages, including the tribulation period and end of the age. We must wrap our minds around the reason Jesus was crucified and understand that we cannot simply attribute it to Israel's transgression. In fact, their transgression has meant riches for the rest of the world (Rom 11:12). For the most part we as Christians have erroneously looked at the persecution and suffering of the Jewish people throughout history as affliction coming from God because of their unbelief and disobedience (As foretold in Deuteronomy 28:62–66), when from God's point of view they are a nation still beloved and dear to him (Rom 11:28). We must change our thinking to conform to God's and view their persecution and suffering as coming from Satan.

When Satan orchestrated the suffering and crucifixion of Christ, he thought he had achieved a victory, but Christ arose. Likewise, when the Jews were driven from their homeland and dispersed among the nations, Satan again believed he had achieved a victory by destroying God's chosen people. But after almost nineteen hundred years passed, he observed that their bloodline still remained, even though they had no nation of their own. It was then that he devised a plan to completely eliminate their bloodline from humanity through an orchestrated event called the Holocaust. Today not only does their bloodline remain but they have also been regathered to their own nation, where Satan will again try to destroy them prior to the beginning of the seven-year tribulation period (Ezek. 38–39). Understanding God's chosen nation is the key to understanding the tribulation period, the end of this age, and the beginning of the new age. "For God's gifts and His call are irrevocable. [He never withdraws them when once they are given, and He does not change His mind about those to whom He gives His grace or to whom He sends His call.]" (Rom. 11:29 AMP).

For over nineteen hundred years, the Jews have been separated from God's plan for them as a nation, but God has called them back home from many nations to complete that plan in this age. As we see them grafted back into what God has planned for them, we find that both Christians and Jews are merging into the same plan, which will lead to the ultimate defeat of Satan and those who serve him as well as the end of this present age.

We must establish a foundation in response to the prophecies Jesus gave to his disciples in Matthew 24 regarding the "last days" and "the day of the Lord" before we can proceed with his foretelling about them. We must be cognizant of the fact that Jesus knew he was about to be "cut off" from the land of the living according to the foreknowledge of God (Dan. 9:26). Israel was also about to be "cut off" from God's plan for them as the result of their transgressions and rejection of the Messiah (Rom. 11:19–22). It is also important for us to comprehend the extent to which Israel had fallen into apostasy, which is the great sin of deliberately turning from God.

Jesus attributed this apostasy to the religious leaders of the day. When Jesus' disciples reported to him that one of his statements had offended the Pharisees, Jesus replied, "Let them alone; they are blind guides of the blind. And if a blind man guides a blind man, both will fall into a pit" (Matt. 15:14 NASB). With these thoughts clearly in mind, we will set the stage for the temporary cutting off of the nation from God's plan by reviewing a few of the activities during the two days before the Passover celebration and Christ's crucifixion (Matt. 26:2).

Jesus and his disciples were on their way to Jerusalem from Jericho to attend and celebrate the Feast of the Passover, which would be held in the next few days. A great multitude followed them, knowing (though many in the city did not) that their long-awaited king, the Messiah, was about to enter the city and the temple, just as the event had been prophesied long ago. The gospel of Luke tells us that when Jesus neared the Mount of Olives and Jerusalem, he experienced a vision of the city being surrounded by armies and hemmed in on every side. When he saw Jerusalem, he wept for the city and the people because they were living in spiritual blindness due to their religious leaders.

> And when he was come near, he beheld the city, and wept over it, saying, If thou hadst known, even thou, at least this thy day, the things which belong unto thy peace! but now they are hid from thine eyes. For the days shall come upon thee, that thine enemies shall cast a trench about thee, and compass thee round, and keep thee in on every side, and shall lay thee even with the ground, and thy children within thee; and they shall not leave in thee one stone upon another; because thou knewest not the time of thy visitation.
>
> —Luke 19:41–44

As Jesus entered the city, the crowd laid their garments down before him, while others cut branches from the trees to cast at his feet. The multitude began crying, "Hosanna to the son of David: Blessed is he that cometh in the name of the Lord" (Matt. 21:9).

The entire city, moved by the sight and by the praises coming from the people, asked the multitude, "Who is this?" (v. 10). Jesus continued to the temple, where he saw the money changers and concluded that the temple of God had been turned from a house of prayer to a commercial enterprise. He overturned their tables and chairs and cast them out of the temple. After he cleared the entryway, many of the blind and the lame came to him, and he healed them. The chief priests and scribes observed all these happenings and were very displeased. Jesus then departed from Jerusalem and lodged in Bethany overnight.

THE APOSTASY OF THE RELIGIOUS LEADERS

The next morning Jesus was hungry. As he approached Jerusalem, he came to a fig tree. But finding only leaves and no figs, he cursed the tree and said, "Let no fruit grow on thee henceforward for ever" (v. 19), and immediately the fig tree withered. Jesus said in John 5:19, "The Son can do nothing of himself, but what he seeth the Father do: for what things soever he doeth, these doeth the Son likewise." It was so with the cursing of the fig tree.

The fig tree was a symbol to Israel of fruitfulness, blessing, and well-being. That's what the word *peace* in Luke 19:42 means. The fruitfulness, blessing, and well-being of the nation were about to wither and die. God the Father had already judged the chief priests and leaders in Israel because they honored their traditions more than God's commandments. They also taught the doctrines of men as if they were the commandments of God. Blind leaders leading blind followers, they were full of pride and whitewashed on the outside, while inwardly they were unclean, spiritually dead, devoid of love, and full of self-righteousness. They did all their works to be seen of men, desiring the best seats in the synagogues and loving to be called "rabbi" (master). Because of them, all in the nation except a remnant walked in darkness. Christians are warned not to "boast . . . at their expense" or to "feel superior" but instead to "stand in awe and be reverently afraid" because "if

God did not spare" them, "neither will He spare [us] [if [we] are guilty of the same offense]" (Rom. 11:18–21 AMP).

A FATHER'S TWO SONS

To illustrate that the age of grace had come to the Gentiles (non-Jewish people throughout the world), Jesus told a story about two sons whom their father had asked to work in his vineyard (Matt. 21:28–32). It was obvious that the two sons represented two nations or people whom God had asked to work in his kingdom. The first son (the nation of Israel) told his father that he would work in the vineyard but later did not. The second son (Gentiles) said he would not work in the vineyard but later regretted his decision and did so. Jesus asked the chief priests and elders who were questioning him about where he had received his authority. "Which of the two did the will of his father?" (v. 31 NASB). They answered that the latter son did. Jesus bluntly told them that the tax collectors and harlots were like the second son; they would enter the kingdom of God before the religious leaders in Israel would.

Jesus immediately followed this story with another vineyard story. This story was even more relevant and clear as to the reason his Father had sent him to earth and to God's plan for the Gentile nations, which would extend from that time well into the tribulation period. In this story Jesus made it absolutely clear that the kingdom of God would be taken from Israel and given to another.

> "Listen to another parable. There was a landowner who PLANTED A VINEYARD AND PUT A WALL AROUND IT AND DUG A WINEPRESS IN IT, AND BUILT A TOWER, and rented it out to vine-growers, and went on a journey. When the harvest time approached, he sent his slaves to the vine-growers to receive his produce. The vine-growers took his slaves and beat one, and killed another, and stoned a third. Again he sent another group of slaves larger than the first; and they did the same thing to them. But afterward he sent his son to them,

saying 'They will respect my son.' But when the vine-growers
saw the son, they said among themselves, 'This is the heir; come,
let us kill him and seize his inheritance.' And they took him,
and threw him out of the vineyard and killed him. Therefore
when the owner of the vineyard comes, what will he do to those
vine-growers?" They said to Him, "He will bring those wretches
to a wretched end, and will rent out the vineyard to other vine-
growers who will pay him the proceeds at the proper seasons."
Jesus said to them, "Did you never read in the Scriptures, 'THE
STONE WHICH THE BUILDERS REJECTED, THIS BECAME
THE CHIEF CORNER stone; THIS CAME ABOUT FROM THE
LORD, AND IT IS MARVELOUS IN OUR EYES'? Therefore I
say to you, the kingdom of God will be taken away from you
and given to a people, producing the fruit of it."

—Matthew 21:33–43 (NASB)

THE ROAD TO APOSTASY

The chief priests and Pharisees understood that he was
speaking about them, and they began to plan how they might seize
him by entangling him in his talk. The Sadducees were the first
group to go to Jesus with their carefully planned questions, but
Jesus answered them with such wisdom that, astonished by his
doctrine, they were silenced. When the Pharisees heard how the
Sadducees had been silenced, they sent a lawyer to tempt Jesus
with this question: "Master, which is the great commandment in
the law?" (22:36). Jesus gave an answer that convicted the lawyer
and the religious leaders of using the law in an unlawful way and
explains how apostasy can take hold.

Thou shalt love the Lord thy God with all thy heart, and with
all thy soul, and with all thy mind. This is the first and great
commandment. And the second is like unto it, Thou shalt love
thy neighbour as thyself. On these two commandments hang
all the law and the prophets.

—Matthew 22:37–40

With this simple response Jesus showed how far the nation had drifted from keeping the commandments God had given to Moses. They were trying to keep the commandments and teaching others to keep them without the motivations of love and faith, as if human effort or works alone would justify them. When giving the first commandment to Moses, God declared that love was the key by saying that he was a God who showed kindness "to those who love Me and keep My commandments" (Ex. 20:6 NASB). When one looks at what God says and sees only "keep My commandments" first, he or she has already adopted a system of works as a way to be accepted by God. But if one first sees "to those who love Me," the focus is on God, and keeping his commandments becomes secondary. In other words man could keep the commandments only out of love for God and others. One cannot obtain love for God and others by keeping the commandments; but if one loves God, keeping the commandments and loving others will come naturally, and keeping them will not be burdensome. To do otherwise is to begin the descent into apostasy. "For this is the message that ye heard from the beginning, that we should love one another" (1 John 3:11).

After the religious leaders left, Jesus turned to his disciples and the multitude, and he began to describe the great apostasy of the scribes and the Pharisees. Religious leaders and all Christians should pay special attention to what Jesus said because 2 Thessalonians 2:3 tells us that this same apostasy, this falling away from loving God, will precede his return (the rapture). Jesus then lists the evidences of apostasy (Matt. 23:4–30) one by one. Among these are the following:

1. Leaders place heavy burdens (system of works) on others but do nothing to remove them.
2. They display their own works to be seen of men, drawing attention to themselves.
3. Religious leaders love to be called "leaders" and "masters." They consider themselves higher than others instead of servants to all.

4. They shut up the entrance to the kingdom of heaven and
   do not enter themselves.

Jesus then tells the religious leaders that their houses will
be left desolate and that they will not see him again until the
day they will say, "Blessed is he that cometh in the name of the
Lord" (v. 39). When Jesus said this, he signified that the day
would come when the Jews would receive him. The apostle Paul
also proclaimed that the day will come when the nation will
accept Christ as their Messiah (Rom. 11:26). He wrote to the
church in Rome that God had not cast away Israel but had only
given them "a spirit (an attitude) of stupor" (v. 8 AMP) "until
the full number of the ingathering of the Gentiles has come in"
(v. 25 AMP). Paul also says that if God did not spare the natural
branches of his olive tree, he also may not spare us because
we have only been grafted into their natural place (vv. 19–21).

JESUS FORETELLS THE END OF THIS AGE

Two days before Passover, Jesus left the temple area and found
a place to sit on the Mount of Olives. The Mount stands to the
east, high above the city and the temple area. It is where the
Messiah's feet will first touch the earth when he returns on the
day of the Lord. When his disciples joined him there, they pointed
out the beauty of the temple. Their words prompted Jesus to say
in Matthew 24:2 that the day would come when not one stone
of the temple buildings would be left on another. The disciples
were alarmed that the temple would be destroyed. They asked
Jesus to tell them when this event would occur, when he would
return again, and when the end of the age would be.

Before we discuss Jesus' answers, it is necessary to begin our
study of the day of the Lord by discussing the end of the age.
We must begin here to understand the events *leading up to* the
tribulation period, the events taking place *during* the tribulation
period, and the events taking place *after* the tribulation period.

This Present Age

The Bible word used for "age" is *aeon* or *aion,* which means a period of time. It could refer to the past, the present, or the future. The *Zondervan Pictorial Encyclopedia of the Bible* says the following about the word *aeon:* "The present age is transitory and evil, its values contrary to those of God; the future age is that in which God holds undisputed sway."[1]

The Beginning and End of this Present Age

The beginning of this present age, as used in the Bible, refers to the period or day when sin and death entered the world in the garden of Eden. On this day Satan became the god of this world and reigned over evil in the world. The present age will end on the day Antichrist is defeated, Satan is bound for a thousand years, and Christ begins to reign in righteousness for a thousand years over all the kingdoms on earth. The day of the Lord will mark the end of this present age and will come after the last trumpet is sounded and announces God's wrath.

The apostle John was raptured in his spirit on the day of the Lord (Rev. 1:10). A voice told him to "write the things which thou hast seen, and the things which are, and the things which shall be hereafter" (v. 19). He was allowed to see the events of the last days, and he saw that great day when the last trumpet will sound, and he wrote what he saw. "And the seventh angel sounded; and there were loud voices in heaven, saying, 'The kingdom of the world has become the kingdom of our Lord and of His Christ; and He will reign forever and ever'" (Rev. 11:15 NASB).

Even after incurring many judgments effecting one third of the world (which will precede God's wrath), the defiled and wicked will not repent of their sorceries, murders, immoralities, or thefts. The age of grace will have ended for those people, and at the sound of the last trumpet, God's angels will pour out seven vials (bowls) of wrath on the earth in the following order:

- Grievous sores will come on those who possess the mark of the beast.
- The sea will turn to thick blood, killing all sea life.
- Rivers and fountains will turn to blood. No one will be able to drink from them.
- Mankind will be scorched with fire and heat, and they will blaspheme God.
- Antichrist's kingdom will be thrown into darkness. People will gnaw their tongues in pain.
- Evil spirits will gather the kings of the world at Armageddon to battle Christ.
- The greatest earthquake in history will divide Jerusalem into three parts and destroy the cities of the world, including Babylon. Every island will disappear, and the mountains will be leveled. One-hundred-pound hailstones will fall on mankind.

We know when and how this present age began, and we can see in the Scriptures how this present age will end. But what do we know about the beginning of the end? The Scriptures indicate that the beginning of the seven-year tribulation period will be the beginning of the end ("the beginning of sorrows" [Matt. 24:8]; also see Luke 21:9). God told Moses—at the time Moses was teaching the statutes to the congregation—that Israel would one day turn from God and be scattered among the nations but that they would return to him *during the time of tribulation.* "When you are in tribulation and all these things come upon you, in the latter days you will turn to the Lord your God and be obedient to His voice" (Deut. 4:30 AMP).

THE SEVEN-YEAR TRIBULATION PERIOD

The Old Testament prophets addressed their prophesying about the tribulation and the day of the Lord to the nation of Israel, and the events they described seem to be mostly concentrated in that nation. To understand when this tribulation period will begin and the nation of Israel will be grafted back into God's plan, we must first understand a vision the angel Gabriel gave to the prophet Daniel for the nation of Israel. The vision concerns seventy weeks, which are actually seventy weeks of years (70 x 7) or 490 years God gave to Israel to fulfill his plan (Dan. 9:24). In the next chapter we will discuss that vision to better understand the response Jesus gave his disciples about when all these things will take place.

CHAPTER TWO

Daniel's Vision

Now I have come to make you understand what is to befall your people in the latter days, for the vision is for [many] days yet to come.

—Daniel 10:14 (AMP)

DANIEL AND HIS people were living as exiles and captives in Babylon because of God's judgment on them. One day as Daniel lay on his bed, he had a dream that contained visions, and the dream left him weak and pale. He understood that four great beasts, which he had seen in the visions, would rise on the earth. He understood that these four great beasts symbolized four great kings, who would establish their kingdoms and extend them over Daniel's people. The beasts in the visions were described as follows and were symbolic of the following kingdoms (Dan. 7:4–7):

First Beast—A lion with wings like an eagle. This beast symbolizes the Babylonian Empire, which was in existence at the time of Daniel's servitude in Babylon.

Second Beast—A bear. This beast symbolizes the Medo-Persian Empire, which was also in existence at the time of Daniel's vision.

Third Beast—A leopard with four birdlike wings and four heads. This beast symbolizes the Greek Empire, which ruled from about three hundred years before Christ and became an empire divided into four parts.

Fourth Beast—A dreadful, terrifying beast with iron teeth and ten horns. This beast symbolizes the Roman Empire, which started ruling in the first century before Christ and ruled during the days of Christ.

These four kingdoms ruled over Israel from the time of King Nebuchadnezzar in Babylon and beyond the time of Christ. The last three of these four kingdoms ruled from about 445 BC when the Jews returned to their homeland from Babylon to rebuild Jerusalem. The last (the Roman Empire) also ruled up to and after the date when Jesus was crucified at about AD 38. No one knows the year when Jesus was crucified or exactly how old he was when he was crucified, but this date satisfies most researchers. The date doesn't really matter because it's only important to know that Jesus was crucified (cut off from the living) after the 483 years, which the angel Gabriel foretold concerning Daniel's vision, had expired, (God had given Israel 490 years to fulfill his plan for them—see following).

We can determine that this timing is so based on what Daniel was told about the Messiah as follows:

Know therefore and understand that from the going forth of the commandment to restore and to build Jerusalem until [the coming of] the Anointed One, a Prince, shall be seven weeks [of years] and sixty-two weeks [of years]. . . . And after the sixty-two weeks [of years] shall the Anointed One be cut off or killed and shall have nothing [and no one] belonging to [and defending Him].

—Daniel 9:25–26 (AMP)

We see from this Scripture that after sixty-nine weeks of years or 483 years (7 x 69 years) the Messiah would be killed. The starting point to count the years is from the going forth of the commandment to restore and build Jerusalem. This

commandment was given to Nehemiah by King Artaxerxes in
Nehemiah 2:1–8. The introduction to the book of Nehemiah in the
Amplified Bible says that Nehemiah came to Jerusalem in 445 BC.

490 YEARS DECREED FOR ISRAEL

The angel Gabriel also told Daniel that God was going to give
the nation of Israel 490 total years to turn from their sins and to
bring in everlasting righteousness according to what he had planned
for them to do in his covenant with Abraham (Gen. 17:6–8). Gabriel
explained,

> Seventy weeks [of years, or 490 years] are decreed upon your
> people and upon your holy city [Jerusalem], to finish and put
> an end to transgression, to seal up and make full the measure
> of sin, to purge away and make expiation and reconciliation for
> sin, to bring in everlasting righteousness (permanent moral and
> spiritual rectitude in every area and relation) to seal up vision
> and prophecy and prophet, and to anoint the Holy of Holies.
>
> —Daniel 9:24 (AMP)

The Jewish people made the full measure of their sin when
they rejected Jesus as their Messiah, which happened in the 483rd
year of the above decree when Jesus was crucified. They have only
seven years remaining in the decree in which "to purge away sin
and make expiation and reconciliation for sin, and to bring in
everlasting righteousness." The decree was put on hold at the time
of Jesus' crucifixion, and seven years remain to fulfill the decree.

This seven-year period is important to understand because
it will also be a time of tribulation that will come on the whole
world. During this seven-year period, God's plan for the Gentiles
and the Jews will begin to merge. The tribulation period will begin
on the day Antichrist confirms a seven-year covenant with Israel,
which will allow them to rebuild their temple and begin offering
sacrifices on the altar in Jerusalem without interference from
other nations. Gabriel told Daniel the following about Antichrist

and the covenant and about when Antichrist would violate the covenant: "And he shall enter into a strong and firm covenant with the many for one week [seven years]. And in the midst of the week he shall cause the sacrifice and offering to cease [for the remaining three and one-half years]" (v. 27 AMP).

After 483 of the 490 years decreed for the nation of Israel passed, God cut them off from his plan because they cut the Messiah off on that date by rejecting and crucifying him. Without their Messiah, they could not fulfill the decree of bringing in everlasting righteousness, sealing up all prophecy, and anointing the Holy of Holies. In the following chapters, we will see how this seven-year period and the plan for Israel all tie together with other scriptures.

The last seven years will not begin until Israel is gathered back to their land (which it now is), until Antichrist as a man of peace confirms that seven-year covenant, and until the Jews begin to offer sacrifices again. They will begin to make expiation for sin when they begin their sacrifices to God. Almost two thousand years have passed since the Jews were cut off from God's plan, but they will be grafted back into his plan when they begin to make amends for their sins by offering sacrifices. Almost two thousand years ago God chose others to carry out his plan.

THE GENTILE NATIONS ARE GRAFTED IN

When Jesus came into the world, he came at the exact time God had ordained, but his people were unprepared. Galatians 4:4–5 tells us this truth. "But when the fulness of the time was come, God sent forth his Son, made of a woman, made under the law, To redeem them that were under the law, that we might receive the adoption of sons."

The Jewish nation was not ready to receive the promise because they had ignored the prophecies of their own prophets. They had not yet brought an end to their sins and transgressions. They were not prepared to usher in righteousness or to receive their Messiah. This lack of preparation didn't cause God to change his plans, only to delay them. His work goes forth at the appointed time, whether mankind is ready or not. He would use this unprepared nation as an example of his severity and mercy for the entire world to see and contemplate. God had another work to do, which had been ordained before the world began, a plan that would mean riches for the rest of the world. None of the princes of this world knew of this plan, "for had they known it, they would not have crucified the Lord of glory" (1 Cor. 2:8).

When Gabriel explained the 490-year period to Daniel, he didn't interrupt it at the end of the 483rd-year period as we are doing now. On the contrary, he continued through the remaining seven years without interruption because the vision was God's plan for Israel alone. When Israel didn't submit to God's plan, however, God delayed his plan for them. This interruption in God's plan is similar to when God tried to lead them from slavery to the Promised Land, as described in the book of Exodus. If they had submitted to God and his plan, they would have arrived at the Promised Land in only eleven days. Because of their rebelling and murmuring against God, however, that generation remained in the wilderness for forty years (Deut. 1:2 AMP). They remained until that generation died and a new generation was born that would enter God's plan.

THE "MYSTERY" OF THE CHURCH

This time, however, the interruption would last much longer. In God's eyes the plan for the nation of Israel was suspended, while his plan for the rest of the world intervened. This plan for the world is the "mystery which hath been hid from ages and from generations, but now is made manifest to his saints" (Col. 1:26). It is the mystery of God's eternal spirit, the Holy Spirit, invading Israel's suspended time period to impart the kingdom of heaven into men's souls. It is the mystery of Christ in us, the hope of glory for the world. It is the mystery of the kingdom of God, dwelling in this world through his church.

Let us take a brief, thoughtful pause here to understand what this mystery is all about before continuing with the time of the "ingathering of the Gentiles" (Rom. 11:25 AMP). Here are several scriptures describing this "mystery":

> And he said unto them, Unto you it is given to know *the mystery of the kingdom of God*: but unto them that are without, all these things are done in parables.
>
> —Mark 4:11 (emphasis mine)

> For I would not, brethren, that ye should be ignorant of *this mystery*, lest ye should be wise in your own conceits; that blindness in part is happened to Israel, until the *fulness of the Gentiles* be come in.
>
> —Romans 11:25 (emphasis mine)

> Now to him that is of power to stablish you according to my gospel, and the preaching of Jesus Christ, according to the *revelation of the mystery, which was kept secret since the world began*, but now is made manifest, and by the scriptures of the prophets, according to the commandment of the everlasting God, made known to all nations for the obedience of faith.
>
> —Romans 16:25–26 (emphasis mine)

> Having made known unto us *the mystery of his will*, according to his good pleasure which he hath purposed in himself: That in the dispensation of the fulness of times he might gather together in one all things in Christ, both which are in heaven, and which are on earth; even in him.
>
> —Ephesians 1:9–10 (emphasis mine)

> For this cause I Paul, the prisoner of Jesus Christ for you Gentiles, If ye have heard of the *dispensation of the grace of God* which is given me to you-ward: How that by revelation he made known unto me *the mystery*.
>
> —Ephesians 3:1–3 (emphasis mine)

That I should *preach among the Gentiles* the unsearchable riches
of Christ; And to make all men see what is the *fellowship of the
mystery*, which from the beginning of the world hath been hid
in God.

—vv. 8–9 (emphasis mine)

Wherefore I am made a minister, according to the dispensation
of God which is given to me for you. . . . *Even the mystery which
hath been hid from ages and from generations*, but now is made
manifest to his saints: To whom God would make known what
is the riches of the glory of *this mystery among the Gentiles;
which is Christ in you, the hope of glory*.

—Colossians 1:25–27 (emphasis mine)

But in the days of the voice of the seventh angel, when he should
begin to sound, *the mystery of God should be finished*, as he hath
declared to his servants the prophets.

—Revelation 10:7 (emphasis mine)

From Luke 21:24 (AMP) we understand that the "times of the
Gentiles" will last until the fullness of the Gentiles has come in.
We understand from Revelation 10:7 that the mystery will end
when the voice of the seventh angel begins to sound. We are
beginning to see that the time of the Gentiles, the mystery, will
extend into the tribulation period, up to the time of the seventh
angel, who has the last trumpet. The seventh angel is the last angel
to sound his voice before the seven bowls of God's wrath will be
poured out on the world. This wrath will be poured out near the
end of the tribulation period. We do not know what the seventh
angel said when he thundered seven times because in Revelation
10:4 the apostle John was told to seal up the things he had said.

PASSING THE TORCH OF THE KINGDOM

By this time the faithful Christians will have run the race
for two thousand years and will have finished their course. In

approximately AD 81 the apostle John was transported in his
spirit to heaven and was allowed to see the future. While in the
spirit on the future day of the Lord, the apostle John saw that
the rapture of the righteous will take place after Jesus opens the
sixth seal of sealed future events (Rev. 6:12; 7:9–17). The rapture
will coincide with the sealing (God's seal of protection) of the
one hundred forty-four thousand servants from the twelve tribes
of Israel. After the rapture some believers who did not make
themselves ready and worthy to meet Christ as well as those
who are not saved and the entire Jewish nation will remain here
on earth.

Along with the one hundred forty-four thousand Jews who
are sealed (protected) will be men and women who believed they
were saved but hadn't prepared themselves, washing their robes
and making them white in the blood of the Lamb (v. 14). They
could also be among the ones who had "fallen away" before the
rapture occurred. They will go through trials to be purified, and
they will be delivered before the wrath of God comes if they do
not take the mark of the beast.

> And some of those who are wise, prudent, and understanding
> shall be weakened and fall, [thus, then, the insincere among
> the people will lose courage and become deserters. It will be
> a test] to refine, to purify, and to make those among [God's
> people] white, even to the time of the end, because it is yet for
> the time [God] appointed.
>
> —Daniel 11:35 (AMP)

God will also seal one hundred forty-four thousand Jewish
believers, and they will minister to the entire Jewish nation,
whom God will shelter and protect during the last three and a
half years of the tribulation period. This matter will be discussed
more fully later.

EVENTS ON EARTH AFTER THE RAPTURE
(THE LAST THREE AND A HALF YEARS)

Once the seventh seal is opened (immediately after the rapture of the righteous and the sealing of believers on earth), seven angels with trumpets will announce the judgments of God (not his wrath) that will come on the earth. The seventh angel will alone announce God's wrath. Notice that even during these first six judgments God will hold back his wrath. These particular judgments will be like warnings to repent before the wrath of God comes. The seven angels will blow their trumpets to announce the following judgments (Rev. 8–9):

First Trumpet—Hail and fire will burn all green grass and one-third of all trees in the world.

Second Trumpet—A burning mountain will fall into the sea, causing one-third of the sea to turn to blood and destroying one-third of sea life and ships.

Third Trumpet—A burning star will fall on one-third of the rivers and fountains on earth. Many will die because the waters will become bitter.

Fourth Trumpet—One-third of the sun, moon, and stars will darken, causing total darkness on one-third of the world during daytime and nighttime.

Fifth Trumpet—Smoke from the bottomless pit will darken the sun and release ferocious locusts and scorpions to torment everyone on earth who do not possess the seal of God, for five months.

Sixth Trumpet—Four fallen angels will be unbound and lead an army of two hundred million mysterious creatures to slay one-third of the world's population. At this point the mystery (Ingathering of the Gentiles) of God will end, and His wrath will begin.

Seventh (Last) Trumpet—The last seven plagues of God will be poured out by seven angels carrying seven bowls of wrath on those who possess the mark of the beast because they will no longer be able to repent. But before the plagues are poured out, the remaining saints on earth who have not taken the mark of the beast will be delivered (see Rev. 15:2).

DANIEL'S VISION OF ANTICHRIST

Daniel's vision of the fourth beast, which symbolizes the old Roman Empire, included an explanation of what would take place within the new, revived (future) Roman Empire in the last days. The old Roman Empire included the most northern part of the continent of Africa, including about half of Egypt and most of Europe, including England, France, Germany, Spain, Italy, and Greece. It also included the Middle Eastern countries of Turkey, Syria, Israel, Jordan, and Iraq.

In his vision Daniel saw that in the last days a little horn would rise out of the ten horns (kings) on that beast (the old Roman Empire). Daniel saw this little horn, Antichrist; pull up three of the ten horns by their roots. Daniel described the little horn as having the eyes of a man, a mouth uttering great boasts, and an appearance that became larger than the other horns. This little horn will persecute the saints during the tribulation period, wearing them down as follows:

> "He will speak out against the Most High and wear down the saints of the Highest One, and he will intend to make alterations in times and in law; and they will be given into his hand for a time, times, and half a time (or three and one-half years)."
>
> —Daniel 7:25 (NASB, explanation mine)

And his power shall be mighty, but not by his own power; and he shall corrupt and destroy astonishingly and shall prosper and do his own pleasure, and he shall corrupt and destroy the mighty men and the holy people (the people of the saints) And

through his policy he shall cause trickery to prosper in his
hand: he shall magnify himself in his heart and mind, and in
their security he will corrupt and destroy many. He shall also
stand up against the Prince of princes, but he shall be broken
and that by no [human] hand.

—8:24–25 (AMP)

PERSEVERANCE OF THE SAINTS

Though God will allow Antichrist to persecute and wear down
the saints both before and after the rapture, the saints will still
be gradually rescuing people out of his kingdom by the word of
their testimony, even during the time they are being persecuted,
imprisoned, and tried in courts. Then at the end of the seven-year
tribulation period, Christ will return on the day of the Lord with
the resurrected and raptured saints. He will destroy Antichrist and
his armies at the battle of Armageddon. An angel explained to
Daniel about the saints overcoming Antichrist: "But the judgment
shall be set [by the court of the Most High], and they shall take
away his dominion to consume it [gradually] and to destroy it
[suddenly] in the end" (7:26 AMP).

The last vision Daniel observed was from a man clothed in
linen, who was girded with fine gold. The appearance of his
body was like a glassy, blue-green color, and his face looked like
lightning. His eyes were like lamps of fire, his arms and feet like
polished brass, and his voice like a multitude speaking. This man
from heaven told Daniel the following:

But thou, O Daniel, shut up the words, and seal the book, even
to the time of the end. . . . And he said, Go thy way, Daniel: for
the words are *closed up and sealed* till the time of the end. Many
shall be purified, and made white, and tried; but the wicked
shall do wickedly: and none of the wicked shall understand;
but the wise shall understand.

—12:4, 9–10 (emphasis mine)

Certain things God had revealed to Daniel were sealed and shut up until the end times. Many years after the resurrection of Christ, the apostle John was rapt in the spirit on the day of the Lord (Rev. 1:10), and he was allowed to see Christ perform the unsealing of these future events. We will now look at what the apostle John was allowed to see concerning the events in these seals. These events will take place during the tribulation period, beginning with the first three and a half years.

CHAPTER THREE

The Seals Are Opened

And one of the elders saith unto me, Weep not: behold, the Lion of the tribe of Judah, the Root of David, hath prevailed to open the book, and to loose the seven seals thereof.

—Revelation 5:5

IN THE YEAR AD 81 the Roman Empire imprisoned the apostle John on the island of Patmos off the coast of Greece because he preached the Word of God and testified about Jesus. During this time in history Christians were being pressured to accept the Roman cult of emperor worship.

John testifies that he was "in the Spirit on the Lord's day" (Rev. 1:10 NASB) and heard a voice telling him to write what he saw in a book and to send the book to the seven churches in Asia. These seven churches, which were in existence at the time of John's writing, represent believers who will be living at the time of the day of the Lord. John was told to write "the things which are, and the things which will take place after these things" (v. 19 NASB).

He saw "one" sitting on a throne in heaven, and in his open hand was a book written on the inside and back, which was sealed up with seven seals (Rev. 5:1 AMP). No one was worthy to open the book until Jesus appeared like a lamb that had been slain; he was found to be worthy to break open the seven seals. As the first five seals were broken open, each appeared to reveal events caused by humans and not as judgments of God until the sixth seal was broken open. When the sixth seal was opened, it revealed God's intervention. Even though God didn't appear to cause the events preceding the opening of the sixth seal, he permitted them to take place. The events appear to be precursors of God's judgments, which follow the sixth seal. The first five seals may be what Jesus described to his disciples in Matthew 24:8 (AMP) as "the early pains" or "the beginning of sorrows" (KJV). The opening of the first six seals (Rev. 6:2–17; 7:9–17) revealed the following events in this order:

1. The First Seal—The Antichrist will receive a crown and go forth to conquer nations.
2. The Second Seal—The world will be thrown into the turmoil of war, and men will slay one another.
3. The Third Seal—The world economy will become inflated, and basic food will become scarce, but oil and wine will be protected.
4. The Fourth Seal—One-fourth of the world's population will die as the result of being slain by men, famine, and wild beasts.
5. The Fifth Seal—Many believers will be killed because of preaching the Word of God and testifying of Jesus.
6. The Sixth Seal—God will intervene for his people by causing a great earthquake, which will cause the sun to become black and the moon to turn red like blood. The stars will fall from the sky, and the sky will split apart and roll up like a scroll. Then every mountain and island will be moved out of their places. All mankind will live in fear, believing that the wrath of God is coming. The resurrected and raptured saints will meet Christ in the air.

At the same time this is happening, God will seal and protect his servants, who will remain on the earth after the rapture of the saints takes place. Four angels will hold back the winds so they won't blow on the earth. Another angel, possessing the seal of

God, will tell the other four angels not to harm the earth or sea until the bond servants of God possess the seal on their foreheads.

John saw the number of those who were sealed, and one hundred forty-four thousand were sealed from the twelve tribes of the sons of Israel. The Bible doesn't say that Gentile believers will be sealed, but 2 Peter 2:9, Psalm 34:7 and Psalm 91:11 promise that they will be protected while their faith is being tried. The time frame of this event (the resurrection, rapture and sealing) is shortly after the midpoint of the seven-year tribulation period. The book of Enoch, also referring to the events of the last half of the tribulation period, says, "But with the righteous He will make peace, and will protect the elect, and mercy shall be upon them."[2] The book of Enoch is not in our Bible, but Jude, the half brother of Jesus, directly quoted a portion from Enoch 1:9 about the day of the Lord in the book of Jude (vv. 14,15).

Then, before Jesus opened the seventh seal, John looked and saw those who had been raptured and resurrected from the earth. John tells us in Revelation 7:9 that he saw "a great multitude" suddenly appear in heaven "clothed with white robes, and palms in their hands." Palm trees have a certain spiritual significance in the Bible. Date palms are described many times as being tall and upright and prized for their dates. Almost every part of the tree can be used for shelter, roofing, fences, and other useful items. The palm tree exemplifies righteousness. Psalm 92:12 tells us, "The righteous shall flourish like the palm tree: he shall grow like a cedar in Lebanon." The following is what John saw and heard:

> After this I beheld, and, lo, a great multitude, which no man could number, of all nations, and kindreds, and people, and tongues, stood before the throne, and before the Lamb, clothed with white robes, and palms in their hands; And cried with a loud voice, saying, Salvation to our God which sitteth upon the throne, and unto the Lamb. . . . And one of the elders answered, saying unto me, What are these which are arrayed in white robes? and whence came they? And I said unto him, Sir, thou

knowest. And he said to me, These are they which came out of the great tribulation, and have washed their robes, and made them white in the blood of the Lamb.

—Revelation 7:9–10, 13–14

The questions that beg to be asked are these: Who are the ones who have washed their robes and made them white? Are they those who claim to have accepted Christ as their Savior, or are they only the ones who have made him Lord and strived to walk in righteousness? Are they only the ones worthy and deserving, as described in Revelation 3:4? The scriptures give us some insight into this.

Wash yourselves, make yourselves clean; Remove the evil of your deeds from My sight. Cease to do evil, Learn to do good; Seek justice, Reprove the ruthless, Defend the orphan, Plead for the widow. "Come now, and let us reason together," Says the Lord, "Though your sins are as scarlet, They will be as white as snow; Though they are red like crimson, They will be like wool. If you consent and obey, You will eat the best of the land; But if you refuse and rebel, You will be devoured by the sword."

—Isaiah 1:16–20 (NASB)

When the rapture comes, those who made themselves ready will be taken. They will be ready for the marriage of the Lamb, even though it does not take place until all the saints are gathered immediately before Christ returns to earth to reign. "'For the marriage of the Lamb has come and His bride has made herself ready.' It was given to her to clothe herself in fine linen, bright and clean; for the fine linen is the righteous acts of the saints" (Rev. 19:7–8 NASB).

Preceding what the apostle Paul wrote about the rapture in 1 Thessalonians 4:16–17, he wrote the following admonition to Gentile believers, spelling out what God expected of them:

For you know what commandments we gave you by the
authority of the Lord Jesus. For this is the will of God, your
sanctification; that is, that you abstain from sexual immorality; that each of you know how to possess his own vessel in
sanctification and honor, not in lustful passion, like the Gentiles
who do not know God; and that no man transgress and defraud
his brother in the matter because the Lord is the avenger in
all these things, just as we also told you before and solemnly
warned you. For God has not called us for the purpose of
impurity, but in sanctification. So, he who rejects this is not
rejecting man but the God who gives His Holy Spirit to you.

—1 Thessalonians 4:2–8 (NASB)

When Jesus broke open the seventh seal, John observed
silence in heaven that lasted about half an hour. This silence
could indicate a time of prayer in heaven for loved ones left
behind (Rev. 8:1, 3–4). The seventh seal, the last seal, begins and
ends the last three and a half years of the seven-year tribulation
period. This period begins with the trumpet judgments previously listed in chapter two.

JOHN'S VISION OF ANTICHRIST

God also gave the apostle John a vision of Antichrist similar
to Daniel's vision. In addition, John also had a vision of the false
prophet. In Revelation 13:1, John described the beast, Antichrist,
as having ten horns with crowns and seven heads, signifying the
kings in his kingdoms. He saw blasphemous names written on
the seven heads. The beast looked like a leopard with feet like a
bear and a mouth like a lion. John understood that Satan was the
one who gave the beast his power and authority. John also saw
that one of the seven heads, the head of Antichrist, was fatally
wounded but healed. The whole world will be amazed by the
beast and follow after him. They will worship not only the beast
but also Satan because Satan will give his authority to the beast,
and no one will be able to make war with him.

God will allow the beast to act with full authority for forty-two months, the last three and a half years of the tribulation period. John observed that he will blaspheme God, God's temple, and those who dwell in heaven. God will also allow him to make war with the saints and to overcome them while they remain on earth. Antichrist's authority will extend over every person and nation in the world.

John saw that only those whose names are written in the Book of Life will refuse to worship Antichrist. He encourages the saints to persevere and have faith during this time. They will see God's swift judgment descend on those who will worship and follow the beast. "He that leadeth into captivity shall go into captivity: he that killeth with the sword must be killed with the sword. Here is the patience and the faith of the saints" (Rev. 13:10).

THE FALSE PROPHET

The false prophet will appear as harmless as a lamb, but he will speak words from Satan. He will cause those on earth to worship the beast (Rev. 13:11–12). Because Antichrist was slain but came back to life, the false prophet will make an image of him to be worshipped. The false prophet will perform many miracles, including causing fire to fall to earth from heaven. He will even cause the image of Antichrist to have breath and speak. He will issue an order that all who do not worship the beast will be killed. To segregate those who worship the beast from those who don't, he will require all people to possess either Antichrist's name or the number of his name on their right hands or on their foreheads. He will also pass a law that those who do not possess this mark cannot buy or sell anything (Rev. 13:16–17).

WARNINGS BEFORE GOD'S WRATH COMES

During the time when Antichrist and the false prophet are requiring all mankind to take the mark of the beast, God will send three angels in "midheaven" (14:6 NASB) with loud voices, and all mankind will hear the following messages:

First Angel

He will appear in "midheaven" to preach the gospel to all mankind in a loud voice, saying, "Fear God, and give Him glory, because the hour of His judgment has come; worship Him who made the heaven and the earth and sea and springs of waters" (v. 7 NASB).

Second Angel

He will follow the first angel, prophesying of the fall of Babylon by saying, "Fallen, fallen is Babylon the great, she who has made all the nations drink of the wine of the passion of her immorality" (v. 8 NASB).

Third Angel

He will follow the first two angels with a warning for all mankind, saying,

> If anyone worships the beast and his image, and receives a mark on his forehead or on his hand, he also will drink of the wine of the wrath of God, which is mixed in full strength in the cup of His anger; and he will be tormented with fire and brimstone in the presence of the holy angels and in the presence of the Lamb. And the smoke of their torment goes up forever and ever; they have no rest day and night, those who worship the beast and his image, and whoever receives the mark of his name.
>
> —vv. 9–11 (NASB)

DELIVERANCE OF THOSE "IN THE LORD"

After the third angel's message, John heard a voice in heaven concerning the restored believers and new believers who refused to receive the mark of the beast, saying: "Write, 'Blessed are the dead who die in the Lord from now on!' 'Yes,' says the Spirit, 'so that they may rest from their labors, for their deeds follow with them'" (v. 13 NASB).

This Scripture does not refer to the Jews who will escape the Antichrist and flee to a place of safety, where God will keep them safe for the last three and one-half years of the tribulation period. At the end of this period these Jews will return to their homeland. The ones spoken of here are the tribulation saints who were not raptured and who will be alive during this period. The deeds that follow them will be their works of faith and courage; they will not lose their reward. Immediately after John heard God order his angels to pour out God's wrath on the earth, he saw the following scene of these believers "in the Lord" who were delivered from the wrath of God because they had not worshipped the beast or taken his mark:

> And I saw something like a sea of glass mixed with fire, and those who had been victorious over the beast and his image and the number of his name, standing on the sea of glass, holding harps of God. And they sang the song of Moses, the bond-servant of God, and the song of the Lamb, saying, "Great and marvelous are Your works, O Lord God, the Almighty; Righteous and true are Your ways, King of the nations! Who will not fear, O Lord, and glorify Your name? For You alone are holy; For ALL THE NATIONS WILL COME AND WORSHIP BEFORE YOU, FOR YOUR RIGHTEOUS ACTS HAVE BEEN REVEALED."
>
> —15:2–4 (NASB)

As we close this chapter with the Scripture about those saints standing on the sea of glass, I am hesitant to reveal the vision of Revelation 15:2–4 I experienced in 1988 while teaching on a Christian TV station. Though I believe the event could happen this way, I'm hesitant because I cannot be sure if the vision came only from my imagination. The vision was short, almost instantaneous. I experienced a very bright splash of pure white light, then the emerging faces of men and women appeared out of the white light. They were standing on a blue, yet almost emerald green, sea of glass. I share my vision only with the reader's understanding that no Scripture I know of can confirm this vision, and it is not prophesied this way in the book of Revelation.

The Bible does tell us, however, that the false prophet will order everyone who doesn't worship the Antichrist to be killed. Take my vision simply as a possibility of the way it *could* happen, not as any kind of prophecy. Here's what I understood from what I saw in my mind:

Those who refused to take the mark of the beast were gathered and taken to a location similar to a concentration camp like the Jews experienced during World War II. The location was a sandy desert. The "sea of glass mixed with fire" (15:2) was a nuclear blast, which melted the sand into glass. My understanding is that those standing on the sea of glass with harps in their hands were translated to heaven at the same instant as the nuclear blast. They experienced no suffering, only deliverance, as evident by their song of praise. Their death and resurrection were instantaneous, and that's why their deeds follow after them. The rewarding of their works comes with no delay because they spent no time in the grave. First Corinthians 15:51 says, "Behold I shew you a mystery; We shall not all sleep, but we shall all be changed."

Other Christians will forfeit their lives during the last three and a half years of the tribulation because of their witness for Jesus, their refusal to worship the beast or his image, and their refusal to take his mark. All believers killed before the wrath of God is poured out will be counted in the first resurrection. John saw Satan being bound for a thousand years and cast into a bottomless pit at the end of the tribulation period. At the same time he saw that these martyred souls will live and reign with Christ for a thousand years.

I saw the souls of them that were beheaded for the witness of Jesus, and for the word of God, and which had not worshipped the beast, neither his image, neither had received his mark upon their foreheads, or in their hands; and they lived and reigned with Christ a thousand years. But the rest of the dead lived not again until the thousand years were finished. *This is the first resurrection*: on such the second death has no power, but they shall be priests of God and of Christ, and shall reign with him a thousand Years.

—Revelation 20:4-6 (emphasis mine)

Before the seven seals were opened, Jesus had messages for the churches that will exist during the day of the Lord. The messages were delivered to the churches in Asia that existed in John's day, but John wrote them in the book of Revelation for us. The next chapter will examine the importance of those messages in great detail.

CHAPTER FOUR

Message to the Churches

Let your light so shine before men, that they may see your good works, and glorify your Father which is in heaven.

—Matthew 5:16

AS PREVIOUSLY NOTED, God gave the apostle John a vision of the day of the Lord. He was told to write everything he saw and heard in a book and to deliver it to the seven churches in Asia or present-day Turkey. The book he wrote is the book of Revelation in our Bible.

The first thing John saw in this heavenly vision was seven golden candlesticks. Jesus was standing in the midst of them, holding seven stars in his right hand. John describes Jesus' appearance as follows:

And in the midst of the seven candlesticks one like unto the Son of man, clothed with a garment down to the foot, and girt about the paps with a golden girdle. His head and his hairs were white like wool, as white as snow; and his eyes were as a flame of fire; And his feet like unto fine brass, as if they burned in a furnace; and his voice as the sound of many waters. And he had in his right hand seven stars: and out of his mouth went a sharp twoedged sword: and his countenance was as the sun shineth in his strength.

—Revelation 1:13–16

Jesus informed John that the seven stars he held in his right hand were seven angelic messengers to the churches and that the seven candlesticks around him were the seven churches. John was told to write down the words Jesus was giving to these messengers and to deliver them to each of these churches. It should be noted that though these particular seven churches existed at the time of John's writing, they symbolize the churches that will exist in the last days. We should also note that these churches were being persecuted and pressured to worship the emperor of Rome, the Roman Empire, and other cults around them. This same pressure will be exerted on Christians in the last days.

Before we study these messages to the churches, it is important for us to understand the significance of the candlesticks.

CANDLESTICKS IN THE BIBLE

Candlesticks are first mentioned in the Bible (Ex. 25:31) when God told Moses to make a candlestick of pure gold with six branches and seven bowls to represent God's communication and light for his people in the tabernacle when Moses led the nation in the wilderness. Each branch held a cup of pure, clear, high-quality olive oil, and the lamps were to burn continuously to give light in the Holy Place. God told Moses to make the candlestick exactly like the pattern God had given. The book of Hebrews tells us why.

> [But these offer] service [merely] as a pattern and as a foreshadowing of [what has its true existence and reality in] the heavenly sanctuary. For when Moses was about to erect the tabernacle, he was warned by God, saying, See to it that you make it all [exactly] according to the copy (the model) which was shown to you on the mountain.
>
> —Hebrews 8:5 (AMP)

God gives us further insight into the importance of the candlestick and its connection to the heavenly sanctuary in the book of Zechariah. An angel awakened Zechariah from his sleep and showed him a heavenly vision. Zechariah responded, "I have looked, and behold a candlestick all of gold, with a bowl upon the top of it, and his seven lamps thereon, and seven pipes to the seven lamps, which are upon the top thereof: And two olive trees by it, one upon the right side of the bowl, and the other on the left side thereof" (Zech. 4:2–3).

Zechariah asked what this vision meant, and the angel explained, "This is the word of the Lord unto Zerubbabel [the governor of Jerusalem], saying, Not by might, nor by power, but by my spirit, saith the Lord of hosts" (v. 6). Then Zechariah asked the angel about the two olive trees by which the golden oil is emptied out. The angel answered, "These are the two anointed ones, that stand by the Lord of the whole earth" (v. 14).

Zerubbabel and Joshua were the governor and priest respectively in Jerusalem at this time. All this imagery is of the angelic messengers, the Holy Spirit, and the two anointed men. All three parties are considered as one in accomplishing God's plan and purpose. God's purpose begins in heaven and is communicated and accomplished on earth. This is the true flow of God. Jesus tells us this in John 10:30, when he says, "I and my Father are one," and this message is repeated again in John 17:21, when Jesus prays that we might be one even as he and his Father are one. This same picture is given to us again in the book of Revelation, where we find the two witnesses. "And I will give power unto my two witnesses, and they shall prophesy a thousand two hundred and threescore days, clothed in sackcloth. These are the two olive trees, and the two candlesticks standing before the God of the earth" (Rev. 11:3–4).

We also understand from these Scriptures that when God speaks about the churches or assemblies, he is not speaking about a building or even groups, but rather about individuals in that assembly who are called to do his work. The reader should consider these messages to the following church assemblies as messages to present-day Christians.

THE ASSEMBLY IN EPHESUS

The apostle Paul established this church and preached there for two years, but at the time of John's writings, it was already becoming an aging church that needed an infusion of the Holy Spirit. The Ephesian believers lived in the midst of worldly people who worshipped idols. Their city's prosperity came from the multitudes who visited the cult temple of Artemis, the goddess of the Greeks, a nature goddess associated with religious sex and prostitution. Ephesians were known for nourishing the spirit of nature. The temple was also a bank, where everyone deposited his or her money.

The Jews had a large colony in Ephesus and enjoyed many privileges in the community. The community was also heavily influenced by the Nicolaitans, who were known to compromise with the surrounding debased cults and they saw the Caesar cult as a harmless loyalty oath, not man worship. This was a society where an easygoing Christianity couldn't survive for long. Jesus acknowledged the church's strengths but also pointed out where they were failing him with a warning for them to repent.[3]

THE MESSAGE (REV. 2:1–7 AMP)

The Lord told the Ephesian church they possessed the Christian quality of "patient endurance" in all their toil and trouble. He recognized they couldn't tolerate wicked people and praised them for their discernment in testing those who called themselves apostles but were really imposters and liars. He also recognized they hated the deeds of the Nicolaitans, which he also hated. He praised them for not growing weary or faint in their activities, but he found one glaring fault: they were trying to do God's will out of duty rather than out of love. Jesus told them, "You have left (abandoned) the love that you had at first [you have deserted Me, your first love]" (Rev. 2:4 AMP).

He then told them that they must repent and do the works they had done when they first loved the Lord. Otherwise he would visit them and remove their lamp stand from its place. The Holy Spirit then addressed the following message to all the churches and modern-day Christians: "He who is able to hear, let him listen to and give heed to what the Spirit says to the assemblies (churches). To him who overcomes (is victorious), I will grant to eat [of the fruit] of the tree of life, which is in the paradise of God" (v. 7 AMP).

THE ASSEMBLY IN SMYRNA

The population in Smyrna had worshipped the deity of the Roman Empire, the emperor, and the Caesar cult for a long time. In AD 26 Smyrna built a temple to Tiberius, which became only the second temple to the deity of Rome in Asia. The Romans oppressed the Christians because they refused to worship Rome. The Jewish synagogue in Smyrna also oppressed the Christians. Polycarp, the bishop of the church in Smyrna, was martyred in AD 155. At the time of his death, he was one of the last remaining pupils of the apostle John.[4]

THE MESSAGE (REV. 2:8–11 AMP)

Jesus confirms in his message to this church that he is aware of their works and tribulation and poverty, but he tells them, "you are rich." Jesus is also aware of the blasphemy coming from the Jewish synagogue and tells the Christians that the "Jews" in the synagogue are not really Jews; they are a synagogue of Satan. He tells them that they are about to suffer and that some of them are about to be put in prison to experience tribulation for ten days. But Jesus tells them to be faithful even unto death, and they will obtain a crown of life. Then the Holy Spirit speaks the following message to all the churches and Christians: "He that hath an ear, let him hear what the Spirit saith unto the churches; He that overcometh shall not be hurt of the second death" (v. 11).

THE ASSEMBLY IN PERGAMUM

The community of Pergamum featured a great altar dedicated to Zeus, the savior (a Greek god), and the people burned incense at the foot of Caesar's statue as worship to the spirit of Rome. The Roman government was so oppressive that Jesus described it as the place "where Satan's throne is." The people also worshiped a god of vegetation. Their coins contained an image of a man raising his hand in a salute, an image adopted by Hitler's Nazi regime. The Christian Antipas was the first to suffer martyrdom in Pergamum for rejecting the emperor worship cult. He died by being burned inside a brazen bull. The Christians were also being influenced by the sect of Nicolaitans within their group, who were always ready to compromise by giving a little pinch of incense before the emperor to show their loyalty to the government. Immorality was evident in the city in the worship of Aphrodite; this immorality was influencing Christian morals.[5]

THE MESSAGE (REV. 2:12–17 AMP)

Jesus tells this church that he knows they are living in a place where Satan is enthroned, yet they are holding fast to his name and have not denied their faith. Jesus is displeased, however, because some members in their midst have set a trap and stumbling block, enticing people to sacrifice to idols and commit sexual sins. Jesus is also displeased because some in their midst cling to the compromising Nicolaitans, a thing God hates. Jesus' last message to them is to repent, or he will come and fight against them.

Then the Holy Spirit gives the following message to all the churches and Christians: "He who is able to hear, let him listen to and heed what the Spirit says to the assemblies (churches). To him who overcomes (conquers), I will give to eat of the manna that is hidden, and I will give him a white stone with a new name engraved on the stone, which no one knows or understands except he who receives it" (v. 17 AMP).

THE ASSEMBLY IN THYATIRA

Thyatira, only twenty miles from Pergamum, had a large Jewish community, and various business guilds in the city demanded social life and pagan rituals. It was difficult to refuse them without losing business and social acceptance in the city. The Nicolaitans in the church were led by a woman John calls "Jezebel," who encouraged the church to compromise with the guilds. Jesus sent her and her associates the message that they were going to go through "great tribulation" if they didn't repent. This church illustrates the "significance of compromise, and apostasy, for the sake of commerce, and trade partnerships with pagan wealth and power."[6]

THE MESSAGE (REV. 2:18–29 AMP)

Jesus acknowledges their love, faith, service, and patient endurance. He also commends them because their recent works are more numerous and greater than their first. Jesus, however, cannot tolerate the woman Jezebel, who claims to be an inspired prophetess but is guiding God's people astray in her teaching, leading them into sexual vice and sacrificing to idols. Jesus has given her time to repent but sees that she has no desire and refuses to do so. The following is God's judgment on her and her followers unless they repent:

> Take note: I will throw her on a bed [of anguish], and those who commit adultery with her [her paramours] I will bring down to pressing distress and severe affliction, unless they turn away their minds from conduct [such as] hers and repent of their doings. And I will strike her children (her proper followers) dead [thoroughly exterminating them]. And all the assemblies (churches) shall recognize and understand that I am He Who searches minds (the thoughts, feelings, and purposes) and the [inmost] hearts, and I will give to each of you [the reward for what you have done] as your work deserves.

—vv. 22–23 (AMP)

To the rest of those in this assembly who have not explored the depths of Satan, Jesus says that he will lay no further burden on them, but they should hold fast until he comes. The Holy Spirit then says the following to all the churches and Christians:

> And he who overcomes (is victorious) and who obeys My commands to the [very] end [doing the works that please Me], I will give him authority and power over the nations; And he shall rule them with a scepter (rod) of iron, as when earthen pots are broken in pieces, and [his power over them shall be] like that which I Myself have received from My Father; And I will give him the Morning Star. He who is able to hear, let him listen to and heed what the [Holy] Spirit says to the assemblies (churches).
>
> —vv. 26–29 (AMP)

We should note that the Holy Spirit promises that the Christians who obey God's commands to the end and do works that are pleasing to God will be given the "Morning Star," who is Jesus. Jesus clearly tells us this in Revelation 22:16, where he states, "I am . . . the bright and morning star." This is a clear reference to the first resurrection and marriage of the Lamb because only those who possess Christ will be resurrected or raptured and will rule the nations (John 11:25).

THE ASSEMBLY IN SARDIS

Sardis was famous for its affluence, gold, and silver coins. But its power and wealth had produced arrogance among its people, and the Christian community had become complacent. The Caesar cult was prominent, and evidence shows that the church may have met in the ancient temple of Artemis.[7]

THE MESSAGE (REV. 3:1–6 AMP)

Jesus tells this church that he knows their record and what they are doing. They are supposed to be alive but in reality are

dead. He tells them to wake up and strengthen what remains
and has not died because he has not found any of their works
that meet God's requirements or that are perfect in his sight. If
they do not repent and prepare for his coming, he will come like
a thief, and they will not suspect the hour when he will return.
Yet in spite of their condition, a few have not soiled their clothes
and still walk with him in white because they are still worthy
and deserving.

Then the Holy Spirit declares the following strong statement
to all the churches:

> Thus shall he who conquers (is victorious) be clad in white
> garments, and I will not erase or blot out his name from the
> Book of Life; I will acknowledge him [as Mine] and I will confess
> his name openly before My Father and before His angels. He
> who is able to hear, let him listen to and heed what the [Holy]
> Spirit says to the assemblies (churches).
>
> —Revelation 3:5–6 (AMP)

The Holy Spirit promises that the names of those who are
victorious in this world will not be erased from the Book of Life.
This is the reason why the Holy Spirit will be able to confess
their names before God and his angels in heaven. Anyone whose
name is not found in the Book of Life will not be saved at the
final judgment.

THE ASSEMBLY IN PHILADELPHIA

This city was located in an area where earthquakes commonly
occurred. An "active synagogue of Jews" there persecuted the
Christians in a culture that was non-Greek and non-Roman.[8]
This absence of Greek and Roman influence signifies that they
were not pressured to conform to the secularism of the Greek
and Roman social orders and that the doors were not closed to
the gospel.

THE MESSAGE (REV. 3:7–13 AMP)

Jesus tells this church that he has set an open door before them that no one is able to shut. He knows they have but little power, yet they have kept his Word, guarded his message, and have not denied him. He tells them that he will make this synagogue of Satan, the Jews who persecute them, come and bow down before their feet and acknowledge that he has loved them. He tells this church that they will escape the tribulation and the hour of trial that is coming upon the whole world because they have guarded and kept his word of patient endurance. He tells them to hold fast to what they have so they may not be robbed of their crown because he is coming quickly.

Then the Holy Spirit says the following to all the churches and Christians:

> He who overcomes (is victorious), I will make him a pillar in the sanctuary of My God; he shall never be put out of it or go out of it, and I will write on him the name of My God and the name of the city of My God, the New Jerusalem, which descends from My God out of heaven, and My own new name. He who can hear, let him listen to and heed what the Spirit says to the assemblies [churches].
>
> —vv. 12–13 (AMP)

THE ASSEMBLY IN LAODICEA

Laodicea was under Roman rule and filled with temples of ancient deities. A large Jewish community there had come from the Babylonian captivity and had been there for a long time; it had been guaranteed freedom of worship. The city was widely known as a banking center and minted its own coins. The citizens were wealthy. This church illustrates the final state of apostasy before the second coming of Christ. According to the *Zondervan Pictorial Encyclopedia of Bible*, this is a classic warning against shortsighted and superficial faith.[9]

The Message (Rev. 3:14–22 amp)

Jesus tells this assembly that they are neither hot nor cold. Because they are lukewarm he will spew them out of his mouth. Though they say in their hearts that they are rich and have need of nothing, they do not understand that they are "wretched, pitiable, poor, blind, and naked" (v. 17). He tells them that they need to be tested by fire like refined gold so they may become truly wealthy. Then they will receive white clothes to keep their nudity from being seen. He also says they need eye salve so they can see. Even in their state of apostasy, he lets them know that he is telling them their faults because he loves them, and that is why he rebukes, warns, and disciplines them. He tells them to become enthusiastic and to repent with burning zeal.

Then the Holy Spirit says the following to all the churches and Christians:

> Behold, I stand at the door and knock; if anyone hears and listens to and heeds My voice and opens the door, I will come in to him and will eat with him, and he [will eat] with Me. He who overcomes (is victorious), I will grant him to sit beside Me on My throne, as I Myself overcame (was victorious) and sat down beside My Father on His throne. He who is able to hear, let him listen to and heed what the [Holy] Spirit says to the assemblies (churches).
>
> —vv. 20–22

It appears that these messages to the churches are directed to the leaders, pastors, teachers, and elders in each congregation. God charges them with the responsibility of leading those they are shepherding to repentance so they might not be part of the great falling away before Christ comes. Within the churches we can see a mixture of true faith and superficial faith. Those of true, sincere faith will be taken at the rapture, but those who fail the test of their faith will be found unworthy to be taken and will need to be tried in the furnace of affliction during the tribulation period, as indicated in this message to the Laodicean church.

We should not consider this trial by fire to be Christ's rejection but rather a time of testing and refining their faith so they might be saved in the end. We find that this judgment of those worthy and unworthy is already taking place in the present-day churches, even as in these churches described in the book of Revelation as follows:

ILLUSTRATIONS OF TODAY'S CHRISTIANS

1. Ephesus—They had fallen into human works and lost their love for Christ. Jesus warned them that if their works were not motivated by love for him, they would not stand the test of worthiness. (We find that some were worthy and overcame, but some did not.)
2. Smyrna—Their suffering and poverty had already made them rich, and they just needed to hold on to what they had to the very end. (These were declared worthy because they had overcome.)
3. Pergamum—Some members were not pleasing to Jesus, and the danger was that these members would lead others astray. Unless they repented, they were destined for the tribulation. If they didn't stand during that time of testing, they would not be saved. (Some were worthy and overcame, and some did not.)
4. Thyatira—Jesus had already judged some of this congregation to be unworthy because they had no desire to repent. Their fate had already been decided or would be decided during the tribulation period. (Some were found worthy and overcame. Some were unworthy because they didn't even desire to repent.)
5. Sardis—This church congregation was spiritually dead, but a few members were found worthy to be taken when Christ returns. Others were in danger of having their

names blotted out of the Book of Life unless they sincerely repented. (Only a few were victorious and worthy—most were not.)

6. Philadelphia—Jesus approved of this assembly and told them that he found their love and works to be worthy of escaping the hour of trial (tribulation) coming on the whole world. (These overcame and were found worthy.)

7. Laodicea—Jesus found this church completely lacking of anything that pleased him because they were lukewarm. Yet he felt that a spark there could ignite a flame if they would repent. This church needed a leader, full of the Holy Spirit, who could ignite the fire. Otherwise they would go through the tribulation period so their suffering might wake them up and regain their faith. Jesus was standing at their door, knocking, and asking to come in. These believers will be unworthy to be taken in the rapture and will be left to go through tribulation, but "tribulation, or distress, or persecution, or famine, or nakedness, or peril, or sword" would never separate them from the love of God (Rom. 8:35).

PROMISES TO THOSE FOUND TO BE WORTHY

Ephesus Promise—Eternal life

Smyrna Promise—Freedom from harm at the final judgment

Pergamum Promise—Hidden manna to eat and a new name to be engraved on a white stone

Thyatira Promise—Granted authority and power to rule over the nations. They would also be given to Christ (The first resurrection).

Sardis Promise—The Holy Spirit will confess their names before God and his angels because the Holy Spirit didn't remove their names from the Book of Life

Philadelphia Promise—A pillar in God's sanctuary and a new name in the New Jerusalem

Laodicea Promise—The honor of sitting beside Jesus on his throne if they opened the door to him

In the next chapter we will examine the government of the revived Roman Empire during the last days and how it will affect the church.

CHAPTER FIVE

Babylon, the Mother of Harlots

I saw a woman seated on a scarlet beast that was all covered with blasphemous titles (names), and he had seven heads and ten horns. . . . And on her forehead there was inscribed a name of mystery [with a secret symbolic meaning]: Babylon the great, the mother of prostitutes (idolatresses) and of the filth and atrocities and abominations of the earth.

—Revelation 17:3, 5 (AMP)

THE BEAST THE woman rode on is Antichrist (see Rev. 13:1–10). One might also surmise that this vision describes her control over Antichrist. An angel informed the apostle John that the seven heads are seven mountains on which the woman sits, (This may be symbolic of seven world kingdoms the harlot has controlled) and the woman herself is the great city Babylon, which reigns over the kings of the earth. The ten horns are also identified as ten kings, who will receive their power during the tribulation period and will accomplish God's will by destroying the harlot in the end (even though they war against God).

Likely the great city described in Revelation 17:5 as "Mystery Babylon" is the city of Rome because the end-time government will rise from the old Roman Empire, whose seat was in Rome. It doesn't follow that the governing religious authority will be the Catholic Church simply because it is located in Rome, but this

48

could happen if the Catholic Church succumbs to the harlot's philosophy.

ANTICHRIST AND THE HARLOT

The harlot, the revived Roman Empire, is a false religion though much more than a religion. It is a philosophy and a system of socio, economic, political, and religious belief all rolled into one. It has been called various names, such as humanism, secularism, progressive liberalism, socialism, and communism, but it is all the same philosophy. Babylon has always been identified as the instrument of Satan, who aspires to mount up to heaven and supplant the living God as the God of this world.

Architects of a new world order (new age movement) have brought this system forth as an alternative to historical religion. These new age architects, who are the power brokers in the world today, support a one-world government and a one-world leader, and they have pledged the world's wealth to accomplish this goal. Through the religion of progressive liberalism, they oppose the Word of God and claim through their feelings to possess more love, compassion, and consideration for humans than God does. They preach equality for all and a golden age of peace and prosperity. Their philosophy seduces people by teaching them to rely on their human feelings instead of on what God says. This philosophy, generally identified today as progressive liberalism and secularism, has permeated society in all nations but especially in Europe. Progressive liberals, who have invaded the Christian churches, are the same as the Nicolaitans in the messages to the seven churches in Asia. They are compromisers of the Word of God. They make the Word of God "of no effect." These hold to the doctrine that Jesus hates (Rev. 2:15).

We find the great harlot of humanism, secularism, and progressive liberalism in our public school system, universities, and public institutions. This system claims to be neutral to religion but in fact aggressively opposes it. The Dictionary defines the characteristics of the great harlot as follows:[10]

Humanism—A philosophy, in which man, his interests, and develop-
ment are made central, and dominant, tending to exalt the cultural,
and rational elements of man, rather than the supernatural or
speculative.

Secularism or Secularize—A regard for worldly, as opposed to spiritual
matters. To make secular; to convert from sacred to secular possession, or uses. To make worldly. To change, (a regular clergyman),
to secular.

Liberal—Characterized by, or favoring policies of reform, and progress,
and generally opposing conservatism, or reaction. Not bigoted, or
prejudiced; broad minded, and not restricted to the literal meaning.
One favoring liberal policies or doctrines, as in politics, religion, etc.

Today's Nicolaitans

Whenever progressive liberals gain control in Christian
denominations or churches, they dismiss the Word of God,
and the church becomes guided by "feelings" rather than by
commandments. These particular churches believe they have
more "feelings" for the oppressed than God does. Their feelings
guide them more than God's Word does. Based on this false belief,
they assume they will be saved in a way they alone understand.
Here are a few examples of progressive liberalism in the church
today:

United Church of Christ—(Not affiliated with the Churches
of Christ, which are undenominational)—It affirms the ideal
that Christians did not always have to agree to live together
in community. This denomination of 1.2 million members has
historically favored progressive or liberal views on gay rights,
women's rights, and other issues.[11] In 1977 the church passed
a resolution which deplored the use of scripture to generate
hatred, and the violation of civil rights of gay and bisexual
persons. This was followed in 1980 by accepting the ordination
of active homosexuals.[12]

The personal feelings of its members can lead the church so far away from God's Word and so pollute it that the church can no longer be considered Christian. Speaking in the context of bad trees that cannot bring forth good fruit and hearts that are filled with evil treasures that bring forth evil, Jesus says, "Why do you call Me, 'Lord, Lord,' and do not do what I say?" (Luke 6:46 NASB).

In addition to the United Church of Christ, progressive liberals have targeted the Episcopal Church, USA.

> Today, there are two religions in the Episcopal Church. One remains faithful to the biblical truth and received teachings of the Church, while the other rejects them.[13]

> [This denomination is currently being split apart.] More liberal Christian denominations have already largely accepted homosexuality as simply another normal, natural, and morally neutral sexual orientation. More conservative denominations have retained the historical Christian belief. They condemn all same-sex behavior, regardless of the nature of the relationship.[14]

Others are guided by personal experiences, their consciences, and reason more than the Bible or dogmas. They don't seem to understand that if they deny the Holy Spirit, they cannot trust their consciences.

These liberal congregations have seemingly little regard for the salvation of the souls of the lost because they approve and applaud their sins. Feigning love, they have become loveless. Pretending to have a heart for the oppressed, they have hardened their hearts to God's Word and can no longer hear the Spirit of God. They seem to fit the definition of those who do not see fit to acknowledge God or approve of him or consider him worth the knowing because they ignore God's righteous decrees concerning homosexuality (Rom, 1:26–27) and exchange the truth of God for a lie (v. 25). Paul writes: "[They were] without understanding, conscienceless and faithless, heartless and loveless [and] merciless. Though they are fully aware of God's righteous decree that those who do such things deserve to die, they not only do them themselves but approve and applaud others who practice them" (Rom. 1:31–32 AMP).

By ignoring God and accepting practicing homosexuals into fellowship without requiring repentance, they are turning the Word of God into a lie. A homosexual is not a "different" person. He is simply a person with the sin of homosexuality, and a person is not a "homosexual" person; he is a sinner. The person can repent of this practice and be delivered, but he must understand that it is sin. This sin is one of several that are an abomination to God (Lev. 18:22, 26), and it is one of the reasons Babylon is called the "Mother of Abominations" in Revelation 17:5. Unbelief in God's Word will cause God to give them up to their own lusts and the consequences of their acts.

> Wherefore God also gave them up to uncleanness through the lusts of their own hearts, to dishonour their own bodies between themselves: Who changed the truth of God into a lie, and worshipped and served the creature more than the Creator, who is blessed forever. Amen. For this cause God gave them up unto vile affections: for even their women did change the natural use into that which is against nature. And likewise also the men, leaving the natural use of the woman, burned in their lust one toward another; men with men working that which is unseemly, and receiving in themselves that recompense of their error which was meet.
>
> —Romans 1:24–27

THE HARLOT—BABYLON, THE MOTHER OF ABOMINATIONS

This harlot, this socio-economic, political, religious government, will corrupt all nations and gain great power through the tribulation period, even power over the Antichrist and the ten kings in his empire. She will believe that her wealth and power are so great that no one can ever pull her down. Revelation 18:7

says, "I sit a queen, and am no widow, and shall see no sorrow."
During this time of power, this government led by Antichrist will
persecute the true Christians, even putting many of them to death.
The harlot will be given the responsibility to distribute goods,
and only those authorized to buy and sell will be able to do so.

When she is destroyed, those who have been made rich by
selling their goods to her will weep and mourn.

> And the merchant's of the earth are waxed rich through the
> abundance of her delicacies. . . . And the merchants of the
> earth shall weep and mourn over her; for no one buyeth their
> merchandise any more. . . . And they cast dust on their heads,
> and cried, weeping and wailing, saying, Alas, alas that great
> city, wherein were made rich all that had ships in the sea by
> reason of her costliness! for in one hour she is made desolate.
>
> —vv. 3, 11, 19

The harlot will be possessed with power given by evil spirits
and will be instructed in her decisions by astrologers, stargazers,
and monthly prognosticators. Her power will grow increas-
ingly great through the incredible wealth of her trade with the
merchants of the world, and Rome (Babylon) will become known
for its luxuries and sensual worldliness. The Antichrist and the
ten kings will resent the harlot, probably because of the harlot's
financial control over them, and God will put into their minds
and hearts the thought of destroying her. Her destruction will
come suddenly and without warning. Before this government
achieves its full power and reaches the pinnacle of wickedness,
however, God will call all his people to come out of her: "I then
heard another voice from heaven saying, Come out from her, my
people, so that you may not share in her sins, neither participate
in her plagues" (v. 4 AMP).

The city of Rome is only fifteen miles from the coastline of
the Mediterranean Sea and the Port of Ostia. In the time of Christ
and the apostles, it was called the "warehouse of the world," and

it was the heart of a vast trading network. The trade at that time included grain, olive oil, wine, spices, gems, silk, and so on; the port was always packed with merchants, ship builders, and officials.[15] These are the same goods that are Mystery Babylon's merchandise in the last days, as listed in Revelation 18:12–13. Since Rome is located on seven hills and only fifteen miles from the Mediterranean Sea, the merchants in ships off the coast will easily see its fiery destruction and the smoke rising forever, as foretold in the book of Revelation. "And every shipmaster, and all the company in ships, and sailors, and as many as trade by sea, stood afar off, And cried when they saw the smoke of her burning, saying, What city is like unto this great city!" (vv. 17–18).

The great harlot system will probably be in existence when the tribulation period begins and will gain power during the first three and a half years. Its destruction will take place sometime during the last three and a half years of the tribulation period at the time when God's wrath is first poured out on the world. Soon after Babylon is destroyed, Jesus and the troops of heaven will descend from heaven to battle the beast, the Antichrist, and the ten kings gathered at the place called Armageddon. Scripture doesn't tell us exactly when that battle will begin or how long it will last.

THE FALSE PROPHET

In Revelation 13, John says that he was standing on a sandy beach and saw Antichrist "coming up out of the sea" (v. 1 AMP). We are also told the false prophet will come up "out of the land" (v. 11 AMP). It is my belief that the Antichrist, coming up on the sandy beach and out of the sea, may be God's way of putting us on notice that the false prophet will try to legitimize the ancestry of Antichrist by connecting him to the throne of David. He might do so by trying to trace his bloodline according to a myth that Jesus and Mary Magdalene had children. This myth, which is not worthy of discussion here, has to do with the old Merovingian myth that is symbolic of Mary Magdalene's crossing the Mediterranean Sea, carrying the child of Jesus, and arriving on the sandy beach coast of Marseilles, France. This fable would give Antichrist a fabricated Jewish heritage though he will probably be a native of Europe. The reference about the false prophet coming up out of the land, however, probably refers to his being a native of the land and having his own ancestral roots in the land of his birth.

Being a false prophet denotes some kind of religious affiliation, which means that he will be part of the harlot's government (Babylon), which will be partly religious. He will posses the same power and control Antichrist will have (Rev. 13:12). They will, in fact, be equal in power. The false prophet will appear meek and innocent like a lamb. However, he will speak powerfully with authority and perform powerful miracles to deceive the world. The following are examples of his power and miracles:

1. He will make fire fall from the sky to the earth.
2. He will perform his miracles in the presence of Antichrist.
3. He will command the inhabitants of the earth to erect a statue or image in the likeness of Antichrist because the Antichrist will be brought back to life after suffering a deadly wound.
4. He will impart the breath of life to the image of Antichrist and cause it to talk.
5. He will put to death those who refuse to bow down and worship the image.
6. He will compel all who wish to buy or sell to be marked or stamped with the name of Antichrist or the number of his name. The human number will be 666.

With all the preceding background information behind us, we can now continue with the answers Jesus gave to his disciples about when these things will "take place, and what will be the signs of [his] coming and of the end" (Matt. 24:3 AMP).

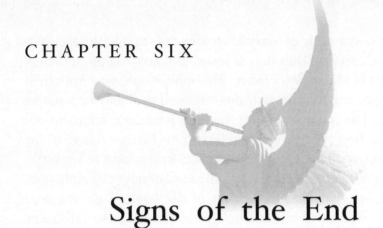

CHAPTER SIX

Signs of the End

When will this take place, and what will be the sign of Your coming and of the end (the completion, the consummation) of the age?

—Matthew 24:3 (AMP)

JESUS BEGAN HIS discourse concerning the signs of his coming by telling his disciples that many people will be led astray. There will be wars and rumors of wars as nations will rise against nations, and famines and earthquakes will occur in many places. But Jesus tells his disciples that all these signs are only the beginning of birth pangs. He then tells his people not to be frightened or troubled when these early signs take place because the end has not yet come. Even though these signs are frightening, Jesus' words bring comfort.

The events Jesus calls in Matthew 24:8 "the beginning of (the early pains) of the birth pangs (of the intolerable anguish)" will coincide with Jesus' opening of the first four seals in heaven (AMP). As we previously discussed in chapter three, John observed the opening of the seals and described what he saw in the book of Revelation as follows:

First Seal—Antichrist will receive a crown.
Second Seal—Peace will be taken from the earth, and men will be slaughtered.

Third Seal—Inflation will occur worldwide, and food shortages will take place.
Fourth Seal—War, famine, disease, and wild animals will kill one-fourth of mankind on earth.

The prophet Isaiah had a vision of these last days when everything mankind has learned to trust in, other than God, will be gradually removed and he writes:

In that day a man shall cast his idols of gold, which they made each one for himself to worship, to the moles and the bats; . . . For behold, the Lord . . . doth take away from Jerusalem and Judah the stay and the staff . . . Say ye to the righteous that it shall be well with him; for they shall eat the fruit of their doings. Woe unto the wicked! It shall be ill with him.

—Isaiah 2:20; 3:1,10

The beginning of birth pangs will end with the killing of one-fourth of the world's population (the fourth seal), and now the birth pangs will come closer as we draw nearer to the day of deliverance.

THE FIFTH SEAL—GOD IS NOT ASHAMED TO BE CALLED THEIR GOD!

It is the opening of the fifth seal that brings anguish and suffering on God's people. Many Christians must give their lives for adhering to the Word of God and for their testimony, but they will not love their lives more than they love God, even unto their death. It is during this time of suffering that Christians will have the greatest opportunity to present the gospel to the entire world. A fulfillment of God's Word in Matthew 24:14 is that the gospel will be preached to the whole world, and then the end will come.

Jesus explains to his disciples that when these days come, Christians will be persecuted and suffer affliction and tribulation. Some will be put in prison, and some will be put to death. All nations of the world will harbor a great hatred of Christians, probably caused by a concentrated propaganda campaign against them. When this hatred and persecution come, they will cause a great falling away of those professed to be Christians. Many Christians today have never faced such hatred, which may come from their own family members. Most have never even considered the prospect of dying for their faith, yet the scriptures have always been clear in this regard, as attested by the following:

> And then many will be offended and repelled and will begin to distrust and desert [Him Whom they ought to trust and obey] and will stumble and fall away and betray one another and pursue one another with hatred.
>
> —Matthew 24:10 (AMP)

> Now the brother shall betray the brother to death, and the father the son: and children shall rise up against their parents, and shall cause them to be put to death. And ye shall be hated by all men for my name's sake: but he that shall endure unto the end, the same shall be saved.
>
> —Mark 13:12–13

> For from henceforth there shall be five in one house divided, three against two, and two against three. The father shall be divided against the son, and the son against the father; the mother against the daughter, and the daughter against the mother; the mother in law against her daughter in law, and the daughter in law against her mother in law.
>
> —Luke 12:52–53

With all the suffering will come grace. Jesus still gives hope and consolation. He says that all this will be a blessing and a time of rejoicing because they will know they are in God's will:

> Blessed are ye, when men shall hate you, and when they shall separate you from their company, and shall reproach you, and

cast out your name as evil, for the Son of man's sake. Rejoice ye in that day, and leap for joy: for, behold, your reward is great in heaven: for in the like manner did their fathers unto the prophets.

—Luke 6:22–23

They will lay their hands on you and will persecute you, delivering you to the synagogues and prisons, bringing you before kings and governors for My name's sake. It will lead to an opportunity for your testimony. So make up your minds not to prepare beforehand to defend yourselves; for I will give you utterance and wisdom which none of your opponents will be able to resist or refute.

—21:12–14 (NASB)

A WINDOW OF OPPORTUNITY

The persecution, suffering, and tribulation endured by God's people will open the door for the gospel presentation. This will be a window of opportunity to bring many to Christ before he returns, but it will not last long. The following Scripture refers to those who will be killed just before the rapture takes place. It is also a reference to those who will be killed after the rapture takes place but before God pours out his wrath:

When the Lamb broke open the fifth seal, I saw at the foot of the altar the souls of those whose lives had been sacrificed for [adhering to] the Word of God and for the testimony they had borne. They cried in a loud voice, O (Sovereign) Lord, holy and true, how long now before you will sit in judgment and avenge our blood upon those who dwell on the earth? Then they were each given a long and flowing and festive white robe and told to rest and wait patiently a little while longer, until the number should be complete of their fellow servants and their brethren who were to be killed as they themselves had been.

—Revelation 6:9–11 (AMP)

The last days for the true Christians could be as glorious as
the first days of the true Christians. Those who are steadfast and
fearless during this time will accomplish great things for the
kingdom of God.

> And the teachers and those who are wise shall shine like the
> brightness of the firmament, and those who turn many to
> righteousness (to uprightness and right standing with God)
> [shall give forth light] like the stars forever and ever.
>
> —Daniel 12:3 (AMP)

> But look to yourselves; for they will turn you over to councils,
> and you will be beaten in the synagogues, and you will stand
> before governors and kings for My sake as a testimony to them.
> And the good news (the Gospel) must first be preached to all
> nations. . . . But say whatever is given you in that hour and at
> the moment, for it is not you who will be speaking, but the
> Holy Spirit.
>
> —Mark 13:9, 11 (AMP)

It will be a similar time as the era of the first Christians, whom
the Roman Empire persecuted in the same way in about AD 100.
Christian historian Philip Schaff writes the following about these
Christians who were persecuted and put to death. His words say
more than I could about a certain grace God gave to our brothers
and sisters.

> To these protracted and cruel persecutions the church opposed
> no revolutionary violence, no carnal resistance, but the moral
> heroism of suffering and dying for the truth. But this very
> heroism was her fairest ornament and staunchest weapon.
> In this very heroism she proved herself worthy of her divine
> founder, who submitted to the death of the cross for the
> salvation of the world, and even prayed that his murderers
> might be forgiven.[16]

The Great Apostasy

Before the day of the Lord comes, many who call themselves Christians will depart from the faith, denying their faith. It will be a sign of the times, a time of lawlessness, hatred, and persecution of Christians. The falling away will happen to those who have weak faith and to those who love the things of this world more than the things of Christ. The following Scriptures give us some insight into how and when this falling away can happen:

Let no man deceive you by any means: for that day shall not come, except there come a falling away first, and that man of sin be revealed, the son of perdition; Who opposeth and exalteth himself above all that is called God, or that is worshipped; so that he as God sitteth in the temple of God, shewing himself that he is God.

—2 Thessalonians 2:3–4

And those upon the rock [are the people] who, when they hear [the Word], receive and welcome it with joy; but these have no root. They believe for a while, and in time of trial and temptation fall away (withdraw and stand aloof).

—Luke 8:13 (AMP)

And the seed which fell among the thorns, these are the ones who have heard, and as they go on their way they are choked with worries and riches and pleasures of this life, and bring no fruit to maturity.

—v. 14 (NASB)

One of the reasons these Christians will fall away is because of false prophets and teachers, who will arise in the last days and deceive many, leading them into error. Another reason is that sin and disobedience to God's Word will cause their love to grow cold and their consciences to be seared. A root of evil, a love of money, in the world can be planted in man's heart, causing him to go astray. "For the love of money is a root of all evils; it is through this craving that some have been led astray and have wandered from the faith and pierced themselves through with many acute [mental] pangs" (1 Tim. 6:10 AMP).

Steadfast Christians have another root that grounds them. It is God's love for them and their love for God that will keep them from falling away during times of trial.

> That he would grant you, according to the riches of his glory, to be strengthened with might by his Spirit in the inner man; That Christ may dwell in your hearts by faith; that ye, being rooted and grounded in love, May be able to comprehend with all saints what is the breadth, and length, and depth, and height; And to know the love of Christ, which passeth knowledge, that ye might be filled with all the fulness of God.
>
> —Ephesians 3:16–19

When sin is unconfessed, it separates us from Christ and causes our love to grow cold. Many Christians will be partakers of the sin and iniquity that will abound in the last days, and they will be separated from the One who is able to keep them from falling. "And the love of the great body of people will grow cold because of the multiplied lawlessness and iniquity" (Matt. 24:12 AMP).

Because of the affliction of the Christians and the persecution by those who hate Christianity, a famine of hearing the true Word of God will occur. The anointed preachers and teachers will be denied a platform to present the gospel, and many will be imprisoned and put on trial. This event will open the door to false prophets and teachers, who will receive a platform and deceive many with false doctrines.

> Behold, the days are coming, says the Lord God, when I will send a famine in the land, not a famine of bread, nor a thirst for water, but [a famine] for hearing the words of the Lord. And [the people] shall wander from sea to sea and from the north even to the east; they shall run to and fro to seek the word of

the Lord [inquiring and requiring it as one requires food], but shall not find it.

—Amos 8:11–12 (AMP)

And many false prophets will rise up and deceive and lead many into error.

—Matthew 24:11 (AMP)

SATAN'S ATTACK BACKFIRES

Cut off from churches and the media, true Christians will be forbidden to preach the Word, causing a famine of hearing the Word of God. The world, however, will be hungry to hear God's Word. Therefore, God will use this time as a unique opportunity to preach the gospel to the entire world. As these Christians are arrested and brought before governing authorities, the authorities will try to humiliate and make an example of them at their trials, probably by broadcasting the proceedings on TV and radio. In this manner the whole world will hear the trial and testimony of the saints. It is the unique plan of God, foretold by Christ in Matthew 24:14, that "this gospel of the kingdom shall be preached in all the world for a witness unto all nations; and then shall the end come."

At these trials the Holy Spirit will give them the words to say, and many listeners in every nation will hear in their own native language and dialect just as they did when the Holy Spirit came on the day of Pentecost. They will be unable to resist the anointed Word of God (Acts 2:6, 11 AMP). They will marvel at the courage, boldness, and faith of the accused, and the truth the Christians speak will stand in stark contrast to the accusations and blasphemy of their accusers. This event will fulfill the prophecy in the book of Daniel that the saints will gradually consume the kingdom of the Antichrist before Christ suddenly destroys it in the end (Dan. 7:26).

Gradually, as the trials progress, it will begin to appear that Antichrist, the false prophet, and his harlot government are on trial; they will stand accused by the Holy Spirit's words and will

convict themselves with their own words. As viewers see and
hear this event, their hearts will begin turning to God. In the
book of Acts, Peter explained to the gathering that what they
had experienced on the day of Pentecost was only the beginning
of what the prophet Joel had prophesied would take place in the
last days.

> And it shall come to pass *in the last days*, God declares, that
> I will pour out of My Spirit upon all mankind, and your sons
> and your daughters shall prophesy [telling forth the divine
> counsels] . . . And I will show wonders in the sky above and
> signs on the earth beneath, blood and fire and smoking vapor;
> The sun shall be turned into darkness and the moon into
> blood before the obvious *day of the Lord* comes—that great and
> notable and conspicuous and renowned [day]. And it shall be
> that whoever shall call upon the name of the Lord [invoking,
> adoring, and worshiping the Lord—Christ] shall be saved.
>
> —Acts 2:17, 19–21 (AMP, emphasis mine;
> also see Joel 2:28–32)

Satan will perceive that Antichrist, considered a man of peace,
has been exposed and revealed as a man of sin. The apostle Paul
prophesied of this day in 2 Thessalonians 2:3, saying, "That day
shall not come, except there come a falling away first, and that
man of sin be revealed." Satan and Antichrist will be infuriated
when their plan backfires on them, and the trials will hasten their
end by exposing their evil, godless, satanic natures. The Jewish
nation will understand that Antichrist is of Satan, and even the
faith of many fallen Christians will be renewed. All this will occur
around the midpoint of the seven-year tribulation period.

This turn of events will alarm Satan, Antichrist, and the false
prophet. Their rage and hatred will intensify against God and his
people. Their frustration will bring about the "abomination of
desolation," foretold by Christ in Matthew 24:15 and the prophet
Daniel in Daniel 11:31. We will discuss this in the next chapter.

CHAPTER SEVEN

The Abomination That Makes Israel Desolate

And I Daniel fainted, and was sick certain days; afterward I rose up, and did the king's business; and I was astonished at the vision, but none understood it.

—Daniel 8:27

ANTICHRIST WILL BE full of rage because he thought putting Christians on trial before the world would diminish and disparage Christ. He will believe that Christians are weak and cowardly, begging for mercy and pleading for their lives before their accusers. By blaspheming God, he will think he can minimize God in the eyes of the world and demonstrate how strong and fearless he is against the power of the Christian God.

Instead people will see the glory of Christ in the faces of the Christians. Instead of cringing cowards, they will see the strength and stability of Christ. Instead of worry or anger, they will see the peace of God in their countenances; the world will recall the day Christ stood before his accusers. Each time a Christian boldly answers his accusers with the words the Holy Spirit provides, they will recognize Jesus when he boldly answered the lawyers with such wisdom that none dared question him again. Without any malice or defiance but with the grace of peace and assurance, the testimony of the saints will overcome Satan. Revelation 12:10 describes how the one who accuses the saints day and night will be cast down to earth: "And they overcame him by the blood of the Lamb, and by the word of their testimony; and they loved not their lives unto the death" (Rev. 12:11).

Satan does not possess patience because that is a fruit of the Holy Spirit. When he is angry and full of hate, he invariably acts hastily, bringing about his own destruction.

The patient endurance of the Christians will expose the Antichrist's evil, satanic nature to the world. Feeling that he must move quickly to overcome this setback, he will order his armed forces to surround Jerusalem and stop the animal sacrifices in the temple. The Bible is clear about when this event will occur—when he breaks the seven-year covenant at its midpoint. "And in the midst of the week he shall cause the sacrifice and offering to cease (for the remaining three and one-half years); and upon the wing or pinnacle of abominations (shall come) one who makes desolate, until the full determined end is poured out on the desolator" (Dan. 9:27 AMP).

THE ABOMINATION

The peak of the abomination that will offend God will occur when the Antichrist takes his seat in the temple and declares he is God. This action will cause Jerusalem and Israel to become deserted and desolate for the remaining three and a half years. The apostle Paul foretells about the great apostasy that will take place prior to Antichrist's being revealed as a man of sin and about how he will respond once he is exposed.

> Let no one deceive or beguile you in any way, for that day will not come except the apostasy comes first [unless the predicted great falling away of those who have professed to be Christians has come], and the man of lawlessness (sin) is revealed, who is the son of doom (of perdition), Who opposes and exalts himself so proudly and insolently against and over all that is called God or that is worshiped, [even to his actually] taking his seat in the temple of God, proclaiming that he himself is God.
>
> —2 Thessalonians 2:3–4 (AMP)

FLEE IMMEDIATELY!

This is the particular event of which Jesus gave a strict warning to his people, Jews and Christians alike, both in Jerusalem and throughout the entire world. When the Antichrist enters Jerusalem with his armed forces, he will most likely have special forces in place all over the world. At his command they will spread out to arrest all Jews and Christians who might oppose him. Their orders will be to capture or kill them to prevent an uprising. In Matthew 24:15–19, Jesus warns his followers that when they see the armies surround Jerusalem, as prophesied in Daniel 11:31, they must immediately leave their homes and workplaces because they will have little time to escape. The time will be reminiscent of Hitler's gestapo forces when they rounded up the Jews in all countries under his control.

> So when you see the appalling sacrilege [the abomination that astonishes and makes desolate], spoken of by the prophet Daniel, standing in the Holy Place—let the reader take notice and ponder and consider and heed [this]—Then let those who are in Judea flee to the mountains: Let him who is on the housetop not come down and go into the house to take anything; And let him who is in the field not turn back to get his overcoat. And alas for the women who are pregnant and for those who have nursing babies in those days!
>
> —Matthew 24:15–19 (AMP)

THE LAST THREE AND A HALF YEARS—THE GREAT TRIBULATION PERIOD

This will be the beginning of a great tribulation period such as the world has never known before. The people of Israel will flee to a place God has prepared for them. There they will be sheltered and safe for the remaining three and a half years. A great sign of a significant future event appeared to the apostle

John in heaven and he saw a symbolic vision of this day. "And the woman [herself] fled into the desert (wilderness), where she has a retreat prepared [for her] by God, in which she is to be fed and kept safe for 1,260 days (42 months; three and one-half years)" (Rev. 12:6 AMP).

The place of safety God has prepared for his people is Petra in the south and perhaps the mountain wilderness to the east of Judea. The Bible doesn't specify a refuge for Christians in various parts of the world, but God promises that this time of affliction will be short. We don't know how long it will last, but presumably it will be only a few days and may coincide with the resurrection of the two witnesses, which will take place in Jerusalem. "And except that the Lord had shortened those days, no flesh should be saved: but for the elect's sake, whom he hath chosen, he hath shortened the days" (Mark 13:20).

Some who are strong and fearless among God's people will rise up to shield and protect those who are fleeing to safety. Others may receive some help from the general population, while still others will give them some support but only from a distance.

> But the people that do know their God shall be strong, and do exploits. And they that understand among the people shall instruct many: yet they shall fall by the sword, and by flame, by captivity, and by spoil, many days. Now when they shall fall, they shall be holpen with a little help: but many shall cleave to them with flatteries.
>
> —Daniel 11:32–34

Those who have previously fallen away and denied the faith will probably not be bothered by the special forces. And others who denied their faith when the affliction begins will probably be set free. Many will regret their decisions and desire to turn back to God, but God will deal with them severely yet with love and compassion since their faith will be tried as by fire during the last three and a half years to purify and save them. "And some of them of understanding shall fall, to try them, and to purge, and to make them white, *even to the time of the end: because it is yet for a time appointed*" (v. 35, emphasis mine).

Because of their hatred of God, collaborators will try to help the forces of Antichrist and gain favors from him. They will hinder and further the distress of those who are fleeing, but God will deal with them accordingly. The Bible gives us examples of God's punishments reserved for these people and nations when it describes the ultimate destruction of Edom, the land of Esau, which will take place on the day of the Lord.

> But thou shouldest not have looked on the day of thy brother in the day that he became a stranger; neither shouldest thou have rejoiced over the children of Judah in the day of their destruction; neither shouldest thou have spoken proudly in the day of distress. . . . Yea, thou shouldest not have looked on their affliction in the day of their calamity, nor have laid hands on their substance in the day of their calamity; Neither shouldest thou have stood in the crossway, to cut off those of his that did escape; neither shouldest thou have delivered up those of his that did remain in the day of distress. For the day of the Lord is near upon all the heathen.
>
> —Obadiah 1:12–15

> Also Edom shall be a desolation; every one that goeth by it shall be astonished, and shall hiss at all the plagues thereof. As in the overthrow of Sodom and Gomorrah and the neighbour cities thereof, saith the Lord, no man shall abide there, neither shall a son of man dwell in it.
>
> —Jeremiah 49:17–18

WAR IN HEAVEN

Another awesome event will take place at the midpoint of the tribulation period at the approximate time or slightly before the abomination of desolation takes place in Jerusalem. The angels of God will go forth to battle Satan and his angels in the heavenly sphere and cast them down to earth.

And there was war in heaven: Michael and his angels fought
against the dragon; and the dragon fought and his angels, and
prevailed not; neither was their place found any more in heaven.
And the great dragon was cast out, that old serpent, called the
Devil, and Satan, which deceiveth the whole world: he was
cast out into the earth, and his angels were cast out with him.

—Revelation 12:7–9

Daniel 7:21–22 implies that Satan and his angels will be
cast out of heaven because God will give judgment in favor of
the saints. Revelation 12:10–11 tells us the reason why: "They
overcame him by the blood of the Lamb and by the word of their
testimony; and they loved not their lives unto death." They were
not afraid to die for their faith. The death of the saints is precious
in the sight of the Lord (Ps. 116:15), and the way they approach
death magnifies Christ. Paul proclaimed in Philippians 1:20–21,
"Christ shall be magnified in my body, whether it be by life, or
by death. For me to live is Christ, and to die is gain."

This event may be what fills the Antichrist with such rage and
hatred of God that he takes his place in the temple and declares
himself to be God. At this time Satan will probably completely
control the Antichrist and not merely influence him. When Satan
sees that he has been cast down to earth, he will immediately
persecute God's people because he knows his time is short. He
will begin with a personal attack on the Jewish people. But when
he sees that God has raised a shield of protection around them,
he will turn his attention to Christians throughout the world.

And when the dragon saw that he was cast unto the earth, he
persecuted the woman which brought forth the man child.
And to the woman were given two wings of a great eagle, that
she might fly into the wilderness, into her place, where she is
nourished for a time, and times, and half a time, from the face
of the serpent. . . . And the dragon was wroth with the woman,
and went to make war with the remnant of her seed, which

keep the commandments of God, and have the testimony of
Jesus Christ.

—Revelation 12:13–14, 17

RECAP OF EVENTS TAKING PLACE DURING
THE FIRST HALF OF THE TRIBULATION PERIOD

Several events will take place during the first three and a
half years of the seven-year tribulation period prophesied by
the prophet Daniel. During this period the first five seals will
be opened, describing signs or events on earth that will take
place. These events will be only warnings or birth pangs, first
preceding the judgments—then the full wrath of God, which is
yet to come. God will give people a chance to repent and prepare
for the rapture. While all this will be happening throughout the
world, another event will occur in Jerusalem.

THE TWO WITNESSES IN JERUSALEM

When the temple is being rebuilt and sacrifices are begun, God
will raise two mighty witnesses who will prophesy in Jerusalem
for three and a half years. They will preach with the power of
Elijah, smite the earth with plagues as Moses did, and dress in
sackcloth like John the Baptist. When adversaries try to capture
or kill them, fire will come out of their mouths and devour them.

The two witnesses will possess miracle-working powers to
keep the rain from falling, to turn the water to blood, and to smite
the earth with plagues whenever they like.

AT THE MIDPOINT OF THE TRIBULATION PERIOD

When the two witnesses are finished declaring their prophecy,
presumably at the midpoint of the tribulation period, Antichrist
will make war with them and kill them. In his pride and arrogance
and in order to appear like God, Antichrist will want the entire

world to see how his superior power prevailed. He will display their dead bodies in the streets of Jerusalem and will not allow them to be buried. TV cameras and reporters will probably be continuously reporting on these dead bodies and the success of Antichrist because the Bible tells us that all "kindreds and tongues and nations shall see their dead bodies" (Rev. 11:9).

This display will continue for three and a half days. People all over the world will rejoice and send gifts to one another because these two witnesses, who had tormented them with prophecies and plagues, are now dead.

THE RESURRECTION

After three and a half days pass, the Spirit of God will enter the dead witnesses, and they will hear a voice from heaven say, "Come up here!" (Rev. 11:12 AMP). When they stand up, great fear will descend on those watching. As their enemies behold them, they will ascend into heaven. Within the same hour a great earthquake will strike Jerusalem, an event that will probably be televised as well. "And the same hour was there a great earthquake, and the tenth part of the city fell, and in the earthquake were slain of men seven thousand: and the remnant were affrighted, and gave glory to the God of heaven" (v. 13 KJV).

Though we cannot state the timing of this resurrection of the witnesses with certainty, it may coincide with the resurrection of all the saints and may simultaneously occur with the rapture of all saints remaining throughout the world. For the Jewish nation, who will flee to safety in the wilderness, this midpoint of the seven-year period will mark the midpoint of Daniel's prophecy concerning the last seven years of the 490-year period when the Jewish people are to accomplish the following: "To make an end of sins, and to make reconciliation for iniquity, and to bring in everlasting righteousness, and to seal up the vision and prophecy, and to anoint the most Holy" (Dan. 9:24).

In Jerusalem the Antichrist and his armies will completely destroy the city and the sanctuary, making it desolate until the end of the remaining three and a half years. As foretold in the book of Daniel, this desolation will be brought about when the Antichrist sits in the temple, declares himself to be God, and stops the sacrifices to God. "And in the midst of the week he shall cause the sacrifice and the oblation to cease, and for the overspreading of abominations he shall make it desolate, even until the consummation, and that determined shall be poured upon the desolate" (v. 27).

The apostle John was told to measure the temple of God and the altar that he saw in his vision but to leave out the court that was outside of the temple because "it has been given to the nations; and they will tread under foot the holy city for forty-two months" (Rev. 11:2 NASB).

SUMMARY OF EVENTS TAKING PLACE AT THE MIDPOINT OF THE TRIBULATION PERIOD

1. War will occur in heaven, Satan and his angels will be cast down to earth.
2. The Antichrist's army will surround Jerusalem.
3. The two witnesses will be killed.
4. The Antichrist will defile the temple, declaring himself to be God.
5. The Antichrist will give the command to arrest or kill the Jews and Christians.
6. The Jewish people will flee to a God-provided place of safety, where they will remain and be kept safe for the remaining three and a half years.
7. The resurrection of the righteous dead (possibly including the two witnesses) and the rapture of the righteous saints will take place.
8. A great earthquake will strike Jerusalem, killing seven thousand people.

In the next chapter we will discuss events happening at the time of the rapture and the resurrection of the saints, which will occur near the midpoint of the tribulation period.

CHAPTER EIGHT

The Rapture

For the Lord himself shall descend from heaven with a shout, with the voice of the archangel, and with the trump of God: and the dead in Christ shall rise first: Then we which are alive and remain shall be caught up together with them in the clouds, to meet the Lord in the air: and so shall we ever be with the Lord.

—1 Thessalonians 4:16–17

"SO SHALL WE ever be with the Lord." We will ever be with the Lord in Paradise (a dwelling place of the righteous dead), which is in the third heaven where Jesus sits on the right hand of the Father. This is the place where the souls of the righteous have been awaiting the day of resurrection to put on their new, glorified bodies. Jesus said there were many homes in his Father's house and that he was going there to prepare a place for us (John 14:2). Then he said, "And when (if) I go and make ready a place for you, I will come back again and will take you to Myself, that where I am you may be also" (v. 3 AMP).

The dead in Christ are not in their graves waiting to be resurrected but in heaven waiting for this day. Their decaying bodies are in the grave, but their souls are in Paradise. Jesus told us so when he told the thief on the cross, who confessed his belief, the following: "Truly I tell you, today you shall be with Me in Paradise" (Luke 23:43 AMP).

The rapture will take place shortly, perhaps even within a few days after the midpoint of the tribulation period, when the Antichrist will take his seat in the temple and declare he is God. Jesus warns his people (Matt. 24:15–20) to flee from their homes, fields, and workplaces when they see the armies of Antichrist surrounding Jerusalem (Dan. 11–31). This event will take place shortly before the rapture. The rapture will occur when the sixth seal is opened in heaven (Rev. 6:12; 7:9–14). Sometimes we forget about the catastrophic signs that will occur on the earth when this event takes place. Everyone's life will be disrupted by great fear when the following occur before and at the time of the rapture and the resurrection of the dead in Christ:

1. The sun will darken, and the moon will become red like blood. The sky will roll up like a scroll, and stars will fall from heaven. Every mountain and island will be moved out of their places (Matt. 24:29; Rev. 6:12–14).
2. In Jerusalem (probably televised), a great earthquake will destroy one-tenth of the city, killing seven thousand people. The two witnesses will be caught up to heaven while people watch (Rev. 11:12–13).
3. The sea and the waves will roar. Men's hearts will fail them because of fear, and they will flee to the dens and rocks in the mountains to hide from God (Luke 21:25–26; Rev. 6:15–17).

The rapture will occur while Christians are suffering affliction and persecution. These catastrophic events will distract the Antichrist's armies from persecuting the Christians for a while. But even with these distractions, every eye will see Christ in the clouds. The Antichrist and all the unsaved will know at this time that Christ's army and God's wrath are soon to come, and they will be even more driven to fight against God and his people. Before these events take place they will come with deceptions and false claims to entice Christians to come out of their hiding places.

Come out, Come out, Wherever You Are

Jesus tells his disciples the Antichrist will send false prophets and teachers to announce that Christ has come, he is in the desert or in secret chambers, and he has returned in a way other than what is prophesied in the Bible. These false prophets will perform great signs and wonders to convince those in hiding that they are genuine prophets to deceive them. Jesus warns his people in Matthew 24:26–27 not to listen to them because when he comes it will be "as the lightning cometh out of the east, and shineth even unto the west."

Distinguishing the Rapture from the Second Coming

Jesus distinguishes between his coming for the resurrection of the righteous dead and those still living at *the midpoint* of the tribulation period and his coming with his army from heaven at *the end* of the tribulation period. He explains that he will descend only to the clouds of the sky, not to earth, at his first coming to gather the saints.

> Then the sign of the Son of Man will appear in the sky, and then all the tribes of the earth will mourn and beat their breasts and lament in anguish, and they will see the Son of Man coming on the clouds of heaven with power and great glory [in brilliancy and splendor]. And He will send out His angels with a loud trumpet call, and they will gather His elect (His chosen ones) from the four winds [even] from one end of the universe to the other.
>
> —Matthew 24:30–31 (amp)

Notice how Jesus describes himself as "the Son of Man" at his *first coming* to gather his people because he is not returning to earth to set up his kingdom at this time. When he returns with his army from heaven *at the end of the tribulation* period, the apostle

John describes him as "King of Kings" because he will establish the kingdom of God at that time.

> His eyes [blaze] like a flame of fire, and on His head are many kingly crowns (diadems): and He has a title (name) inscribed which He alone knows or can understand. He is dressed in a robe dyed by dipping in blood, and the title by which He is called is The Word of God. And the troops of heaven, clothed in fine linen, dazzling and clean, followed Him on white horses. . . . And on His garment (robe) and on His thigh He has a name (title) inscribed, KING OF KINGS AND LORD OF LORDS.
>
> —Revelation 19:12–14, 16 (AMP)

THOSE WHO ARE READY

Jesus concludes his discourse about the signs of his coming for his people, which will take place in the midst of their affliction, with the following words: "Watch ye therefore, and pray always, that *ye may be accounted worthy* to escape all these things that shall come to pass, and to stand before the Son of man" (Luke 21:36, emphasis mine).

"That ye may be accounted worthy"! What does Jesus mean by this phrase in his reference to the rapture? Jesus immediately begins teaching in parables, indicating who will and will not be accounted worthy to be taken in the rapture. He begins the parables by referring to himself as a man going on a long journey and leaving work for his servants to do while he is gone. Each generation has its own work:

> For the Son of man is as a man taking a far journey, who left his house, and gave authority to his servants, and to every man his work, and commanded the *porter* to watch. Watch ye therefore: for ye know not when the master of the house cometh, at even, or at midnight, or at the cockcrowing, or in the morning: Lest

coming suddenly he find you *sleeping*. And what I say unto you I say unto all, Watch.

—Mark 13:34–37 (emphasis mine)

An important symbol used in the above parable is the word *porter*. The Bible uses this word to describe a gatekeeper or someone who guards the door. The Bible refers to Jesus as the door. "I am the door: by me if any man enter in, he shall be saved, and shall go in and out, and find pasture" (John 10:9). Jesus is the Door to the kingdom of heaven, and the Porter or Doorkeeper, therefore, is the Holy Spirit, who has been sent to convict the world of sins and to give gifts to men in furtherance of God's kingdom. Jesus tells the disciples to watch that they do the work that has been given for them to do and that the Holy Spirit will be guarding the door to heaven so only those the Lord finds so doing will be found worthy to enter heaven when he returns.

Another symbol in the parable is the word *sleeping*. Sleeping, other than normal sleep in the Bible, usually refers to death, either physical death or spiritual death. Sleep is a state of darkness or unawareness, and those who are spiritually dead or sleeping do not have the light by which to walk, as illustrated by the following Scripture: "Awake thou that sleepest, and arise from the dead, and Christ shall give thee light" (Eph. 5:14).

Those sleeping are those who have stopped bearing fruit because they have become disconnected from the light and walk in darkness. The next parable explains it this way: "I AM the True Vine, and My Father is the Vinedresser. Any branch in Me that does not bear fruit [that stops bearing] He cuts away (trims off, takes away); and He cleanses and repeatedly prunes every branch that continues to bear fruit, to make it bear more and richer and more excellent fruit" (John 15:1–2 AMP).

Many Christians today believe they can do God's work in their own human wisdom and strength without a vital union and close relationship with Christ. By vital union and close relationship, we are speaking of prayer, communion, and brotherly love, which result in righteous living. By fruit we mean the fruit of the Holy Spirit, as listed in the following Scripture: "But the fruit of the Spirit is love, joy, peace, longsuffering, gentleness, goodness, faith, meekness, temperance: against such there is no law" (Gal. 5:22–23).

Pursue Love! Make It Your Great Quest

The Holy Spirit flows from the vine to the branches, keeping them alive and causing them to bear fruit. Jesus concludes the passage in John 15:1–5 by saying, "However, apart from Me [cut off from vital union with Me] you can do nothing" (v. 5 AMP). The Christian may not be casting out demons, healing the sick, or performing miracles, but his or her life should evidence the fruit of the Holy Spirit if there is vital union with Christ. Notice that the first fruit mentioned in Galatians 5:22 is love. Love is vital because "God is love" (1 John 4:8 AMP).

Only love can motivate us to keep and do the Lord's commandments. Without love we cannot keep the commandments; in fact, they become burdensome. Listen to what love is and understand how keeping the commandments is easy and natural when one has love.

God's Love

Love endures long and is patient and kind; love never is envious nor boils over with jealousy, is not boastful or vainglorious, does not display itself haughtily. It is not conceited (arrogant and inflated with pride); it is not rude (unmannerly) and does not act unbecomingly. Love (God's love in us) does not insist on its own rights or its own way, for it is not self-seeking; it is not touchy or fretful or resentful; it takes no account of the evil done to it [it pays no attention to a suffered wrong]. It does not rejoice at injustice and unrighteousness, but rejoices when right and truth prevail. Love bears up under anything and everything that comes, is ever ready to believe the best of every person, its hopes are fadeless under all circumstances, and it endures everything [without weakening].

—1 Corinthians 13:4–7 (AMP)

SINS MUST BE CONFESSED

Once we understand what Christ expects from his elect, we begin to understand his teaching about who will be taken in the rapture and who will remain for the tribulation, described as the furnace of fire when there will be weeping and gnashing of teeth (Matt. 13:42, 50). Just as we can know the fruit of the Spirit, which are evidences of righteousness, we can also recognize the fruits of the flesh, which are evidences of unrighteousness. Paul's letter to the Galatians makes it clear that "those who do such things shall not inherit the kingdom of God" (Gal. 5:21 AMP). The doings of the flesh are the following:

immorality	jealousy	carousing	impurity	anger
indecency	selfishness	idolatry	divisions	sorcery
factions	enmity	envy	strife	
drunkenness				

When a believer recognizes any of these doings in his or her life, he or she should confess them to God, who will then restore that vital union and grant power to overcome them.

JUDGMENT BEGINS IN THE HOUSE OF GOD

For the time is come that judgment must begin at the house of God: and if it first begin at us, what shall the end be of them that obey not the gospel of God? And if the righteous scarcely be saved, where shall the ungodly and the sinner appear? Wherefore let them that suffer according to the will of God commit the keeping of their souls to him in well doing, as unto a faithful Creator.

—1 Peter 4:17–19

The rapture is not the time of final judgment for those who are not ready or for the unsaved. It is only a time for the resurrection of the righteous and the deliverance of those judged worthy. The Lord will not reject or abandon those who are not judged to be worthy at the time of his coming; instead he will purify them and make them worthy during the time of tribulation—their trial by fire. God purifies his people from sin by chastisement, suffering, and affliction to the point that sin is no longer attractive to them. This is God's plan, and those who are impure should rejoice in it because they can accomplish great works during their time of suffering. The following Scriptures help us understand how we come to be vitally united with Christ through righteous suffering:

> For he that hath suffered in the flesh hath ceased from sin; That he no longer should live the rest of his time in the flesh to the lusts of men, but to the will of God.
>
> —vv. 1–2

> For I reckon that the sufferings of this present time are not worthy to be compared with the glory which shall be revealed in us.
>
> —Romans 8:18

> Who shall separate us from the love of Christ? shall tribulation, or distress, or persecution, or famine, or nakedness, or peril, or sword? As it is written, For thy sake we are killed all the day long; we are accounted as sheep for the slaughter. Nay, in all these things we are more than conquerors through him that loved us.
>
> —vv. 35–37

> For even hereunto were ye called: because Christ also suffered for us, leaving us an example, that ye should follow in his steps. . . . Who, when he was reviled, reviled not again; when he suffered, he threatened not; but committed himself to him who judgeth righteously.
>
> —1 Peter 2:21, 23

Now no chastening for the present seemeth to be joyous, but grievous: nevertheless afterward it yieldeth the peaceable fruit of righteousness unto them which are exercised thereby.

—Hebrews 12:11

THE SEPARATION

Jesus tells us that he will send forth his angels to gather his elect, the worthy, as they separate the unrighteous from the righteous. The separation in his house will first be a separation of the unsaved from the saved, the false from the true. Jesus tells another parable, explaining why this is necessary when he gives the parable of the wheat (true believers) and the tares (false believers). "But while men slept, his enemy came and sowed tares among the wheat, and went his way. But when the blade was sprung up, and brought forth fruit, then appeared the tares also" (Matt. 13:25–26). Jesus then says, "Let both grow together until the harvest" (v. 30).

JUDGE NO MAN

When men sleep (are in darkness) is when the unbelieving and workers of iniquity mingle with believers. Tares represent false believers who mingle with true believers. It is the "bringing forth of the fruit" that identifies the tares when compared to the fruit brought forth by the wheat. God is careful not to pass judgment on the wheat and the tares until the day of the harvest comes; he also tells us not to pass judgment. God warns us not to pass judgment on others because he alone knows the hearts of men and women. "Therefore judge nothing before the time, until the Lord come, who both will bring to light the hidden things of darkness, and will make manifest the counsels of the hearts" (1 Cor. 4:5).

He tells us that if we judge, we might pull up some of the wheat with the tares. This judgement and separation will take place on the day of the rapture. "The Son of man shall send forth his angels, and they shall gather out of his kingdom all things that offend, and them which do iniquity; And shall cast them into a furnace of fire: there shall be wailing and gnashing of teeth. Then shall the righteous shine forth as the sun in the kingdom of their Father" (Matt. 13:41–43).

THE BAPTISM OF FIRE

When the angels cast those who offend and those who do iniquity into the furnace of fire, this act is not a casting into hell as some may suppose. Rather it describes leaving them to go through a trial (baptism) by fire during the tribulation period. Matthew 3:11 tells us that Jesus will baptize us not only with the Holy Spirit but also with fire. Jesus also went through this same baptism. In Luke 12:50, he says, "But I have a baptism to undergo, and how distressed I am until it is accomplished" (NASB). The "wailing and gnashing of teeth" is an expression of their severe disappointment, disbelief, and distress that they were not taken in the rapture. This group of people will consist of those who were never truly saved but were falsely led to believe they were. The group will also include those who were truly saved but fell away from faith because of the world's severe persecution and hatred of Christians. The Lord will deem them unworthy to enter the kingdom of heaven at the time of the rapture because they turned away from following him. "No man, having put his hand to the plough, and looking back, is fit for the kingdom of God" (Luke 9:62).

In all this separation we must never forget that Jesus is an advocate before the Father for all believers, whether they have made themselves ready for the rapture or not. This separation does not cut them off from his love for them.

THE JEWS, GOD'S CHOSEN PEOPLE

God will leave both groups, fallen believers and unbelievers, to endure the tribulation, but he will give them a chance to

repent: the fallen believers to prove their faith and unbelievers
to be saved. The gospel will still be preached during this period.
Even the Jews, who will be safely hiding in the wilderness and at
Petra, will hear the gospel preached by the one hundred forty-four
thousand believing Jews (twelve thousand from each of the twelve
tribes). They possess the seal of God on them and follow Jesus
wherever he leads. Before the Jews fled to safety, the prophetic
words of the two witnesses in Jerusalem will also be fresh in their
minds. The last words of the Old Testament prophet Malachi
foretold the coming of Elijah, represented by the two witnesses,
to turn the nation back to God. The Jewish nation will have the
following as witnesses:

The Prophets

"Behold, I will send you Elijah the prophet before the coming
of the great and dreadful day of the Lord: And he shall turn the
heart of the fathers to the children, and the heart of the children
to their fathers, lest I come and smite the earth with a curse"
(Mal. 4:5–6).

The Second Coming

"And they shall look [earnestly] upon Me Whom they have
pierced, and they shall mourn for Him as one mourns for his only
son, and shall be in bitterness for Him as one who is in bitterness
for his firstborn" (Zech. 12:10 AMP).

The Trial by Fire—Tribulation

And it shall come to pass, that in all the land, saith the Lord,
two parts therein shall be cut off and die; but the third shall be
left therein. And I will bring the third part through the fire, and
will refine them as silver is refined, and will try them as gold is
tried: they shall call on my name, and I will hear them: I will
say, It is my people: and they shall say, The Lord is my God.

—13:8–9

As it is with the Jewish people, so will it be with the Gentiles left behind, except the Jews will return to Israel as a nation *after* God's wrath is poured out. But believing and purified Christians will be raptured or resurrected *before* the wrath of God is poured out. None of these Jews or the believing and purified Christians will endure God's wrath.

THE GENTILES, GOD'S OTHER SHEEP

Suffering and persecution will continue during the last half of the tribulation period as God's six pre-wrath judgments will fall upon the world. These judgments are not the wrath of God; rather, these judgments, which will impact one-third of the world, are designed to bring people to repentance. Furthermore, God's grace will continue to help those who undergo the trial and the proving of their faith. God will not allow them to be tried more than they can endure, and they will possess the promise God gives to those who patiently persevere: "But he that shall endure unto the end, the same shall be saved" (Mark 13:13).

This period, the three and a half years after the rapture, will also include a time when the false prophet and the Antichrist will force people to take the mark of the beast if they want to buy or sell. They will not succeed in forcing everyone to do so because they will not have enough manpower throughout the world to police this measure. Many will heed the warning by the angel flying in "midheaven" and will flee to avoid taking the mark. However, the majority will take the mark willingly. Christians who refuse to do so will be easily identified, targeted, and probably be taken to concentration camps of some sort. The final salvation of Christians who refuse to take the mark will come immediately before the last trumpet sounds and God pours his wrath on the earth. The following Scripture refers to those who die "in the Lord" before the wrath of God takes place:

Their Salvation

A third angel flying in "midheaven" will loudly announce that the wrath of God is coming and will warn those on earth that they will incur God's wrath and eternal torment if they worship the beast and take his mark (Rev. 14:9–11). Then John spoke a word of encouragement for the saints who are still in the world at this time:

> "Here is the patience of the saints: here are they that keep the commandments of God, and the faith of Jesus." John then heard a voice from heaven telling him to write, "Blessed are the dead which die in the Lord from henceforth: Yea, saith the Spirit, that they may rest from their labours; and their works do follow them."
>
> —Revelation 14:12–13

These saints will be resurrected to heaven before the wrath of God is poured out on the world and will be counted as part of the first resurrection (see Rev. 20:4-6).

The salvation of those left behind during their hour of trial (the last Christians) is represented in the parable Jesus told about the laborers a man hired to work in his vineyard; they all agreed to work for a penny a day. Some were hired early in the morning, some in the third hour, some in the sixth hour, and some in the ninth hour. In the eleventh hour he found other laborers standing around because no one would hire them, so the Lord hired them for whatever was right. At the end of the day he paid the laborers, starting with the last unto the first. The last laborers received the same wages for their work as the first. Those who had worked more hours murmured because the ones who had worked only one hour (the hour of trial that was to come on the whole world—Rev. 3:10) received the same wages, even though they hadn't worked as long. Then the Lord told the laborers, "Friend, I do thee no wrong: didst not thou agree with me for a penny? . . . Is it not lawful for me to do what I will with mine own? Is thine eye evil, because I am good? So the last shall be first, and the first last: for many be called, but few chosen" (Matt. 20:13, 15–16).

In many of Jesus' parables he hints that only half of those who believe will be taken in the rapture, while half will be left behind. In Matthew 24:40–41, he says, "Then shall two be in the field; the one shall be taken, and the other left. Two women shall be grinding at the mill; the one shall be taken, and the other left." He told another parable about Christians who grow tired of waiting for his return and fall back into worldliness.

> But and if that evil servant shall say in his heart, My Lord de-layeth his coming; and shall begin to smite his fellowservants, and to eat and drink with the drunken; the lord of that servant shall come in a day when he looketh not for him, and in an hour that he is not aware of, and shall cut him asunder, and appoint him his portion with the hypocrites: there shall be weeping and gnashing of teeth.
>
> —vv. 48–51

Another parable Jesus told concerns those who are wise and those who are foolish. When the Bible speaks of the wise in this parable, it relates to those who are wise to do good (see Rom. 16:19). The foolish are those who do not obey God's Word (see Ps. 5:5 and Matt. 7:26). In Galatians 3:3, Paul tells the Galatians they are foolish because they started their walk with the Holy Spirit but then tried to be perfect by depending on their own flesh and wisdom. The following parable about ten virgins who took their lamps and went out to wait for the bridegroom to come has many spiritual symbols:

Oil=The Holy Spirit
Lamp=The Word of God
Virgins=Born-again Christians
Bridegroom=Christ
Announcement of his coming=The signs of his coming
Door=Jesus is the Door to heaven.

Then shall the kingdom of heaven be likened unto ten virgins, which took their lamps [the Word of God], and went forth to meet the bridegroom [Christ]. And five of them were wise [obedient], and five were foolish [disobedient]. They that were foolish took their lamps, and took no oil [Holy Spirit] with them: But the wise took oil in their vessels with their lamps. While the bridegroom tarried, they all slumbered and slept [were unaware]. And at midnight there was a cry made, Behold, the bridegroom cometh: go ye out to meet him. Then all those virgins arose, and trimmed their lamps. And the foolish said unto the wise, Give us your oil; for our lamps are gone out. But the wise answered, saying, Not so; lest there be not enough for us and you; but go ye rather to them that sell, and buy for yourselves. And while they went to buy, the bridegroom came; and they that were ready went in with him to the marriage: and the door was shut. Afterward came also the other virgins, saying, Lord, Lord, open to us. But he answered and said, Verily I say unto you, I know you not. Watch therefore, for ye know neither the day nor the hour wherein the Son of man cometh.

—Matthew 25:1–13

Jesus then tells about a man who traveled to a far country and left his goods with his servants according to the abilities of each, to oversee for him. Before he left he entrusted to one servant five talents (a sum of money), to another two talents, and to another one. While he was gone the servant with five talents used them wisely and doubled the amount entrusted to him. The servant with two talents also doubled the amount. But the servant who possessed one talent buried it in the ground to keep it safe.

When the lord returned, he told the servants who had used the talents profitably that they had done well; he would make them rulers over even more. He, however, severely rebuked the servant who had hid his talent and removed the talent entrusted to his care and gave it to the other servants. The lord then threw the unprofitable servant into outer darkness where there was weeping and gnashing of teeth (paraphrased from Matt. 25:14–30).

This parable is not about money or investments but about spiritual, ministry, and service gifts God bestows to accomplish His ordained purpose or work for each person in every generation. The servant who hid his talent should stir up visions of the Christian who attends church every week but continues to live for the world, doing nothing to further God's kingdom.

The parables Jesus gave to his disciples are not references to the final judgment. This will not happen until the great white throne judgment, which will take place after Christ's thousand-year reign on earth. God gave these parables to show that some will be found worthy to be taken when the Lord comes in the clouds, and some will be left to be purified before God pours his wrath out on the earth.

Those tried in the furnace of the tribulation, the hour of trial, will come forth like purified gold; they will be saved and taken to heaven. Then—and only then—will God's wrath be poured out on all the inhabitants of the earth who have refused to repent.

The next chapter will show what will happen when first the judgments followed by the wrath of God come upon the earth after the rapture and during the remaining three and a half years of the tribulation period.

CHAPTER NINE

Judgments and Wrath

Or do you think lightly of the riches of His kindness and forbearance and patience, not knowing that the kindness of God leads you to repentance? But because of your stubbornness and unrepentant heart you are storing up wrath for yourself in the day of wrath and revelation of the righteous judgment of God, who WILL RENDER TO EVERY MAN ACCORDING TO HIS DEEDS.

—Romans 2:4–6 (NASB)

WE DO NOT know exactly when the wrath of God will begin, but we do know that it will begin and end before the close of the seven-year tribulation period. We know this because of Daniel's vision that the Jewish people will anoint a Holy of Holies (Daniel 9:24), an act that will end the final seven-year period ordained for that nation to bring in everlasting righteousness. The most Holy Place is in Jerusalem, and the Jews will be unable to anoint it until the completion of God's wrath and the defeat of Antichrist and his armies.

God's wrath will be preceded by the six judgments of God. These judgments will begin after the rapture, which will take place shortly after the first three and a half years of the seven-year tribulation period. The Bible says that silence in heaven for about a half an hour (When the saints will pray—Rev. 8:3–4) will occur after the rapture and before the judgments. The time period the first six judgments will cover is called the "hour of trial." We will refer to the time of God's wrath as the "hour of wrath." The Bible sometimes uses the word *hour* to mean a literal hour, a short time, or a season.

We find the reference to the "hour of trial" in the Lord's message to the church in Philadelphia; he promised to keep these believers from the time of the judgments. In other words he will find them worthy to be taken in the rapture. "Because you have guarded and kept My word of patient endurance [have held fast the lesson of My patience with the expectant endurance that I give you], I also will keep you [safe] from the *hour of trial (testing)* which is coming on the whole world to try those who dwell upon the earth" (Rev. 3:10 AMP, emphasis mine).

Another reference to "hour" as a short time period is what we call the "hour of wrath," which refers to when the ten kings give their power to the Antichrist in order to make war against Christ and his saints. "And the ten horns which thou sawest are ten kings, which have received no kingdom as yet; but receive power as kings *one hour with the beast*. These have one mind, and shall give their power and strength unto the beast. These shall make war with the Lamb, and the Lamb shall overcome them" (17:12–14, emphasis mine).

THE "HOUR OF TRIAL"—JUDGMENTS FROM GOD

The wrath of God will not come until God knows that everyone who will repent has done so. Before his wrath comes he will send judgments on one-third of the world; these are designed as signs or warnings to bring sinners to repentance. Listed in Revelation 8–9, these six judgments before the wrath of God comes are referred to as the "trumpet judgments." The rapture will occur when Jesus opens the sixth seal, which will take place three and a half years into the tribulation period. Then after the rapture (midpoint of the tribulation period) Jesus will open the seventh seal, which will contain all the trumpet judgments including the seventh, which will contain God's wrath.

During the first six judgments God will send three angels flying in "midheaven." The first angel will preach the eternal gospel to every nation and warn them to fear God because his judgments have come. The second angel will warn that Babylon has fallen. The third will warn all mankind not to take the mark of the beast and to refuse to worship his image; otherwise they will partake of God's wrath and be tormented in the lake of fire (Rev. 14:6–10). During these judgments God will give mankind one last chance to repent.

> Collect your thoughts, yes, unbend yourselves [in submission and see if there is no sense of shame and no consciousness of sin left in you], O shameless nation [not desirous or desired]! [The time for repentance is speeding by like chaff whirled before the wind!] Therefore consider, before God's decree brings forth [the curse upon you], before the time [to repent] is gone like the drifting chaff, before the fierce anger of the Lord comes upon you—yes, before the day of the wrath of the Lord comes upon you! Seek the Lord [inquire for Him, inquire of Him, and require Him as the foremost necessity of your life], all you humble of the land who have acted in compliance with His revealed will and have kept His commandments; seek righteousness, seek humility [inquire for them, require them as vital]. It may be you will be hidden in the day of the Lord's anger.
>
> —Zephaniah 2:1–3 (AMP)

The prayers of the saints, (possibly for loved ones left behind), will precede the six pre-wrath trumpet judgments during the half an hour of silence in heaven. Then the angels will pour the judgments out, each on one-third of the earth as follows (Rev. 8:1–13; 9:1–21, AMP):

1. Hail and fire, mixed with blood, will burn up one-third of the green grass and trees.
2. A burning mountain will fall into the sea, causing one-third of the sea to turn to blood and destroying one-third of sea life and ships.

3. A meteor will fall on one-third of the rivers and springs, poisoning them and causing many deaths.
4. One-third of the sun, moon, and stars will be darkened, causing darkness for one-third of both day and night.
5. Smoke from the bottomless pit will darken the sun and air, bringing forth locust-like scorpions to torment mankind (for five months) who do not have the seal (protection) of God on their foreheads. Men will seek death but are not permitted to die.
6. Four angels who were bound will be released from the Euphrates River and lead two hundred million horsemen to kill one-third of mankind with plagues, fire, and brimstone from their mouths.

THE LAST CALL

The Lord of love and mercy will issue one last call to the world before the angels pour out his wrath, which will be contained in the seventh and last trumpet judgment. "Therefore also now, saith the Lord, turn ye even to me with all your heart, and with fasting, and with weeping, and with mourning: And rend your heart, and not your garments, and turn unto the Lord your God: for he is gracious and merciful, slow to anger, and of great kindness, and repenteth him of the evil" (Joel 2:12–13).

THE "MYSTERY" OF THE LAST TRUMPET

There is no doubt that the seventh angel, who has the seventh trumpet, which contains the seven bowls of God's wrath, will conclude a "mystery" because the Bible tells us so. "But in the days of the voice of the seventh angel, when he is about to sound, then the mystery of God is finished, as He preached to His servants the prophets" (Rev. 10:7 NASB).

The seventh trumpet will be the "last trumpet," which will release God's wrath. It will not be sounded until all God's people are safe. The Jews will be safe in a place God prepared for them, and all Gentile believers will be safely taken to heaven. Jesus has made it clear that the resurrection and rapture will take place after the Antichrist is revealed as a man of sin and the abomination of desolation takes place in Jerusalem. The book of Daniel makes it clear that the abomination of desolation will take place at the midpoint of the seven-year covenant with Israel. The book of Revelation shows the resurrection and rapture taking place when the sixth seal is opened after the events of the first five seals.

Yet one particular Scripture causes some people trouble when they place the rapture at the midpoint of the tribulation period. The timeline of this Scripture seems to indicate the rapture may not occur until the *last* trumpet sounds. They correctly believe the *last* trumpet refers to the *seventh* trumpet in the book of Revelation, which will announce God's wrath, and they assume this Scripture refers to the rapture. Here is the Scripture causing the confusion: "Take notice! I tell you *a mystery* (a secret truth, an event decreed by the hidden purpose or counsel of God). We shall not all fall asleep [in death], but we shall be changed (transformed) In a moment, in the twinkling of an eye, *at the [sound of the] last trumpet call.* For a trumpet will sound, and the dead [in Christ] will be raised imperishable (free and immune from decay), and we shall be changed (transformed)" (1 Cor. 15:51–52 AMP, emphasis mine).

If the rapture takes place at the time of the seventh trumpet, that timing would place the rapture near the end of the tribulation period. Let us carefully note what the apostle Paul *is* saying and is *not* saying in this Scripture. First and foremost, this same Paul wrote what is perhaps the best description of the resurrection and the rapture in another letter, 1 Thessalonians 4:15–17. His description there agrees exactly with what Jesus told his disciples and says nothing about the last trumpet. As a matter of fact, many glaring differences exist between what the apostle Paul wrote in 1 Thessalonians and what he wrote in 1 Corinthians. Let us carefully examine what he wrote in 1 Thessalonians before we compare the two:

THE RAPTURE

For this we declare to you by the Lord's [own] word, that we
who are alive and remain until the coming of the Lord shall
in no way precede [into His presence] or have any advantage
at all over those who have previously fallen asleep [in Him in
death]. For the Lord Himself will descend from heaven with a
loud cry of summons, with the shout of an archangel, and with
the blast of the trumpet of God. And those who have departed
this life in Christ will rise first. Then we, the living ones who
remain [on the earth], shall simultaneously be caught up along
with [the resurrected dead] in the clouds to meet the Lord in
the air; and so always (through) the eternity of the eternities)
we shall be with the Lord!

—4:15–17 (AMP)

THE TWO SCRIPTURES, TWO DIFFERENT EVENTS

When we carefully compare the two Scriptures, we see that
they don't appear to be describing the same event. In 1 Thessalonians Paul writes about those "who are alive and remain
until the coming of the Lord" (4:15 NASB). First Corinthians
15:51 simply speaks of "some who will not fall asleep in death"
and does not mention the time being "at the coming of the
Lord" (NASB) as 1 Thessalonians 4:15 does. When the seventh
angel sounds his trumpet, the last trumpet, in 1 Corinthians
15:52, he will announce the seven bowls of wrath described in
Revelation 11:15–19, not the coming of the Lord, which is what
1 Thessalonians describes. First Thessalonians 4:15 refers to the
resurrection of those who have previously "fallen asleep" and are
dead; in contrast, 1 Corinthians 15:51 refers to those who "shall
not sleep but will be changed." First Thessalonians 4:16–17
refers to Jesus descending from heaven, where the saints will be
caught up together in the clouds to meet the Lord in the air. First
Corinthians doesn't even mention Jesus or his descending from
heaven. Furthermore, Jesus doesn't descend from heaven to the

earth at the last trumpet sound; he comes back later after all the bowls of wrath have been poured out. First Thessalonians refers to being caught up together in the clouds; 1 Corinthians 15:52 says only that they will be changed in a moment, which will be when the last trumpet sounds. The last trumpet will release the seven bowls of wrath to come on the earth (Rev. 15:1). Jesus does not descend to earth until the last bowl of wrath is poured out, when he returns with his saints for the battle of Armageddon (Rev. 19:11–15). Perhaps the most important difference is that Paul in 1 Corinthians 15:51 refers to this change as being a "mystery" but says nothing about a "mystery" in 1 Thessalonians.

The Rapture Is Not a Mystery

In 1 Thessalonians Paul doesn't describe the resurrection and rapture as being a mystery because Jesus had already described the rapture exactly the way it would happen to his disciples. Paul begins 4:15 declaring his description is according to the "Lord's own word," and this was a known fact to all the disciples, not a mystery. Paul refers to the event as a "mystery" in the letter to the Corinthians because it was an event decreed to take place that had not yet been disclosed. It would not be disclosed until it was disclosed by Paul and was shown by the apostle John many years later, which he would write about in Revelation 10:7, and describe in greater detail in 15:2–3, which was revealed to John and which he wrote after Paul died.

This "mystery" or event is neither a resurrection from the grave nor a rapture of the living. This event is when the last remaining Gentile believers on earth, who refuse to take the mark of the beast, will die without experiencing the sleep of death or the grave. Instead they will be changed in the twinkling of an eye *at the moment of death*. This change will take place when the seventh angel begins to sound his trumpet, the last trumpet, and immediately before the wrath of God begins. John described what he saw when the "mystery of God is finished," which is when the seventh angel will sound his trumpet, as described in Revelation 10:7.

At the sound of the last trumpet, immediately before God's wrath begins, John saw the deliverance of the last Christians (the final ingathering of the Gentiles), exactly as Paul describes it in 1 Corinthians 15:51–52. John writes, "And I saw as it were a sea of glass mingled with fire: and them that had gotten the victory over the beast, and over his image, and over his mark, and over the number of his name, stand on the sea of glass, having the harps of God. And they sing the song of Moses the servant of God, and the song of the Lamb" (Rev. 15:2–3). It seems that these people do not fall asleep in death but are changed in a moment, as the last trumpet begins to sound. This event is much later, and the description is different from the great multitude no one could count from all nations, which John saw suddenly appear in heaven after the sixth seal was opened in Revelation 7:9 (the rapture).

The Hour of Wrath

The time of trial and testing at this point is over, and the seventh trumpet judgment, the last trump, brings the wrath of God because the rest of mankind, who have not been killed refuse to repent:

> The rest of rebellious mankind, who were not killed by these plagues, did not repent of the works of their hands, so as not to worship demons, and the idols of gold and of silver and of brass and of stone and of wood, which can neither see nor hear nor walk; and they did not repent of their murders nor of their sorceries nor of their immorality nor of their thefts.
>
> —9:20–21 (NASB)

The seventh or last trumpet judgment brings the wrath of God. This judgment consists of seven bowls or vials of wrath that God will pour out on the earth as follows:

First Bowl—Poured out on mankind, causing grievous sores to appear on those bearing the mark of the beast and on those who worshipped his image.

—16:2

Second Bowl—Poured out on the sea, causing it to turn to putrid blood and killing everything in the sea.

—v. 3

Third Bowl—Poured out on all the rivers and fountains, turning them to blood.

—v. 4

Fourth Bowl—Poured out on the sun, causing it to scorch men with fire so they blaspheme God's name.

—vv. 8–9

Fifth Bowl—Poured out on the headquarters of Antichrist, causing his kingdom to fall into darkness and bringing sores and pain on men so they gnaw their tongues in anguish and blaspheme God.

—vv. 10–11

Sixth Bowl—Poured out on the Euphrates River, drying it up so evil spirits go forth to gather the kings of the earth to battle on the day of the Lord. They gather them in a place called Armageddon.

—vv. 12–16

Seventh Bowl—Poured into the air, causing thunder, lightning, and the greatest earthquake the earth has ever known. This earthquake will divide Jerusalem into three parts and cause the cities of other nations to fall. The great city of Babylon will be completely destroyed. Every island will disappear, and every mountain will be leveled. Large, heavy hailstones will fall from heaven, and mankind will blaspheme God.

—vv. 17–21

BABYLON'S DESTRUCTION

Babylon is a great city, the seat of government that will reign over the kings of the earth, just as the city of Rome ruled over the kings in its empire during the days of Christ. The angel with the seven vials of wrath showed the apostle John the destruction of Babylon. It is hard to know exactly how this destruction will come about, but the Bible tells us that God will put it into the hearts of the ten kings of Antichrist to accomplish it. The destruction seems to take place just after the kings and their armies are gathered in a place called Armageddon in preparation for the battle with Christ. It may occur after the great earthquake takes place; the armies may come to take spoils from the city.

John was shown that "her plagues [shall] come in one day, death, and mourning, and famine; and she shall be utterly burned with fire" (Rev. 18:8). "And in her was found the blood of prophets, and of saints, and of all that were slain upon the earth" (v. 24). The city will rule over the ten kings, and they will hate her. The final destruction, which is burning by fire, will take place at the hands of these ten kings because God will put it into their hearts to do so. "And the ten horns which thou sawest upon the beast, these shall hate the whore, and shall make her desolate and naked, and shall eat her flesh, and burn her with fire. For God hath put in their hearts to fulfil his will, and to agree, and give their kingdom unto the beast, until the words of God shall be fulfilled" (17:16–17).

Jeremiah 51 prophesies about the destruction of Babylon and of all those who dwell in the midst of her. Before the wrath of God comes, people will be warned to flee the evil Babylonian system to save their souls. The Bible says that Babylon will be abundant in treasures of all kinds. It is prophesied in Jeremiah

51:53 that "spoilers" will come unto her from the north. We read that rumors of invaders coming against Babylon will be spread a year before the destruction occurs. And in the following year it will take place.

> My people, go ye out of the midst of her, and deliver ye every man his soul from the fierce anger of the Lord. And lest your heart faint, and ye fear for the rumour that shall be heard in the land; a rumour shall both come one year, and after that in another year shall come a rumour, and violence in the land, ruler against ruler.
>
> —Jeremiah 51:45–46

> Though Babylon should mount up to heaven, and though she should fortify the height of her strength, yet from me shall spoilers come unto her, saith the Lord.
>
> —v. 53

> And they [of Babylon] shall be dismayed and terrified, pangs and sorrows shall take hold of them; they shall be in pain as a woman in childbirth. They will gaze stupefied and aghast at one another, their faces will be aflame [from the effects of the unprecedented warfare].
>
> —Isaiah 13:8 (AMP)

When the wrath of God has passed, the geography of the world will have changed forever. Cities will be no more, the great mountain ranges will be leveled and the waters made blood. Desolation will be upon the world! Everything not of God will have been shaken, and only those things that cannot be shaken will remain. The world will see the fulfillment of Christ's words when he said, "And when the flood arose, the stream beat vehemently upon that house, and could not shake it: for it was founded upon a rock" (Luke 6:48). It will also be a fulfillment of the following prophecies:

But now he hath promised, saying, Yet once more I shake not the earth only, but also heaven. And this word, Yet once more, signifieth the removing of those things that are shaken, as of things that are made, that those things which cannot be shaken may remain.

—Hebrews 12:26–27

I will make a man more precious than fine gold. . . . Therefore I will shake the heavens, and the earth shall remove out of her place, in the wrath of the Lord of hosts, and in the day of his fierce anger.

—Isaiah 13:12–13

For thus saith the Lord of hosts; Yet once, it is a little while, and I will shake the heavens, and the earth, and the sea, and the dry land; And I will shake all nations, and the desire of all nations shall come: and I will fill this house with glory, saith the Lord of hosts.

—Haggai 2:6–9

However, the shaking is not yet over because the day of the Lord is still to come, as we shall see in the next chapter.

CHAPTER TEN

The Day of the Lord

*And it shall come to pass in that day, that the light shall not be
clear, nor dark: But it shall be one day which shall be known to the
Lord, not day, nor night: but it shall come to pass, that at evening
time it shall be light.*

—Zechariah 14:6–7

THE DAY OF the Lord will be a day like no other since the
beginning of time. Those on earth will awaken to a dark, gloomy
morning. The light from the sun will be obscured, and visibility
will be low. These will be the survivors of the greatest earthquake
the earth has ever known, and darkness will hide the wasteland
and desolation surrounding them.

A sense of foreboding will hang over the remaining inhabitants, especially over the armies of the kings gathered together in
the place called Armageddon. A feeling of doom will permeate
the air. They must fight or they must die. When they die, their
death will be final and in everlasting torment.

They gather in anticipation of the great day of the Lord,
and now they will wait. Reports reach the camp of incredible
destruction caused by the earthquake felt around the world.
The great, manmade skyscrapers have crashed and crumbled;
entire mountain ranges have been leveled, and the oceans have
completely covered the islands. The entire earth has been razed,

and only sparse populations remain. They and their huge army are left to fight God. Hatred and blasphemy fill the camp, and their impatience grows as they are forced to wait for the day of the Lord. "Woe to you who desire the day of the Lord! Why would you want the day of the Lord? It is darkness and not light; It is as if a man fled from a lion and a bear met him, or went into the house and leaned with his hand against the wall and a serpent bit him. Shall not the day of the Lord be darkness, not light? Even very dark with no brightness in it?" (Amos 5:18–20 AMP).

The days drag on, and suspense builds in the camp. What time is it? There is neither noon time nor evening, only gray gloominess. There is neither light nor darkness. It is not a normal day; it is a time period known only to God. Unemotional, fearless, and hardened soldiers begin to weep in the camp as the truth begins to sink in that they are not the invaders or the aggressors. Rather, they are the invaded awaiting the invasion. The stench of dung permeates the camp, enhancing the feeling of helplessness. "The great day of the Lord is near, it is near, and hasteth greatly, even the voice of the day of the Lord: the mighty man shall cry there bitterly. That day is a day of wrath, a day of trouble and distress, a day of wasteness and desolation, a day of darkness and gloominess, a day of clouds and thick darkness" (Zeph. 1:14–15).

The Jewish community, which had been safe in Petra and in the wilderness of other countries, has returned to Jerusalem to survey the ruins of their beloved city and the temple. They have heard the great trumpet prophesied by the prophet Isaiah. "And it shall come to pass in that day, that the great trumpet shall be blown, and they shall come which were ready to perish in the land of Assyria, and the outcasts in the land of Egypt, and shall worship the Lord in the holy mount at Jerusalem" (Isa. 27:13). The armies of the Antichrist, tired of waiting, have begun moving toward Jerusalem to annihilate those who have emerged from their hiding. The armies have become full of fearless warriors again as they near Jerusalem. The waiting is over. A battle cry sounds in the city, and the Jews are alarmed because there are no escape routes.

Suddenly from the vast darkness comes a shout. Like rolling thunder, it echoes around the earth. A distant, rumbling sound like a tornado follows the shout, and all eyes turn to the dark sky. A small, bright light appears in the distant darkness. It grows larger and brighter until it fills the sky.

> And Enoch also, the seventh from Adam, prophesied of these, saying, Behold, the Lord cometh with ten thousands of his saints, To execute judgment upon all, and to convince all that are ungodly among them of their ungodly deeds which they have ungodly committed, and of all their hard speeches which ungodly sinners have spoken against him.

> —Jude 1:14–15

> For, behold, the day cometh, that shall burn as an oven; and all the proud, yea, and all that do wickedly, shall be stubble: and the day that cometh shall burn them up, saith the Lord of hosts, that it shall leave them neither root nor branch. But unto you that fear my name shall the Sun of righteousness arise with healing in his wings; and ye shall go forth, and grow up as calves of the stall. And ye shall tread down the wicked; for they shall be ashes under the soles of your feet in the day that I shall do this, saith the Lord of hosts.

> —Malachi 4:1–3

THE RETURN

The Lord will descend on the Mount of Olives as the armies approach Jerusalem. The Mount of Olives will split in half from the east to the west. On the day Jesus ascended into heaven after his resurrection from the dead, he ascended into heaven from the same Mount of Olives. As his disciples watched him ascend into the clouds, an angel appeared and foretold this day of the Lord. "Ye men of Galilee, why stand ye gazing up into heaven? this same Jesus, which is taken up from you into heaven, shall so come in like manner as ye have seen him go into heaven" (Acts 1:11).

When the Mount of Olives splits from east to west, a "very great valley" will be created, and half of the mountain will move toward the north and half toward the south (Zech. 14:4). This shift will open a route of escape from Jerusalem in the day of Christ when he does battle with the Antichrist (Zech. 14:3–5). The battle itself may take place in Jerusalem and spill over into this newly created "very great valley"; the Bible doesn't say that the battle will actually occur at Armageddon. It says only that the army of the kings will gather in a place called (in the Hebrew tongue) Armageddon. The Hebrew word simply means "to gather" or "a gathering place." The prophet Zechariah says in Zechariah 14:5 that the very great valley will reach unto Azal, but Azal cannot be identified. There is some indication, however, that the valley could reach a distance of two hundred miles, extending through modern-day Jordan to the Syrian desert.

The battle will be great, and we do not know how long it will last. Some of the supernormal bodies of the saints may be thrust through during the battle, but they will be unharmed. The following Scripture indicates that the Antichrist's army will enter Jerusalem and cause havoc before the Lord and his army confront them in battle. "For I will gather all nations against Jerusalem to battle, and the city shall be taken and the houses rifled and the women ravished; and half of the city shall go into exile, but the rest of the people shall not be cut off from the city. Then shall the Lord go forth and fight against those nations" (vv. 2–3 AMP).

THE ARMY OF THE LORD

The armies of the nations may outnumber the troops of heaven, but they will be no match for the Lord's army. To understand the supernormal army of the Lord, we must understand what a resurrected body is. From the scriptures we can establish what the new spiritual body will be like. First, it will not be a spirit like God the Father or the Holy Spirit, but it will be a combination of flesh, bones, soul, and spirit.

The resurrected or transfigured body will be like Jesus' resurrected body. The scriptures tell us in Luke 9:32 that his body was glorious. When Jesus suddenly appeared before his disciples after rising from the dead, they thought they were seeing a spirit. He convinced them that he had flesh and bones, explaining that a spirit lacks these. Showing them his hands and feet, he told them that he possessed bones, but he didn't say he had blood. He also showed that he could eat by consuming a piece of fish and a honeycomb.

Those who knew him didn't immediately recognize his resurrected body because he no longer bore his earthly image; he had put on a heavenly image. The following Scripture gives us a descriptive picture of what a glorious body looks like when Peter, James, and John followed Jesus to a high mountain, where he met and talked with Moses and Elijah. They appeared from their heavenly home to talk to Jesus, who was transfigured in their presence. "And his face did shine as the sun, and his raiment was white as the light" (Matt. 17:2).

From the following Scriptures, we know that our resurrected or changed bodies will possess the following characteristics:

1. It will be an actual body of flesh with bones, hands, and feet. It will shine brightly and gloriously (Job 19:26; Ezek. 37:5; Matt. 17:2; Luke 24:39; Phil. 3:21).
2. It will be like the bodies of the angels and of Christ (Ps. 17:15; Matt. 22:30; Luke 20:36; 1 John 3:2).
3. It will be a spiritual body, not just an invisible spirit (Mark 16:12; 1 Cor. 15:42, 44, 49).
4. It will be able to eat and drink (Matt. 26:29; Luke 24:51).
5. It will be able to travel between earth and heaven (Luke 24:51; Acts 1:9).
6. It will be clothed in white linen, clear and bright (Matt. 17:2; Rev. 7:9; 19:8, 14).
7. Those in resurrected and transfigured bodies will not marry; they will be like the angels (Matt. 22:30).
8. They will never die (Luke 20:36).

Those in the army of God will live in supernormal, resurrected bodies.

THE BATTLE

The book of Joel gives the best description of this army in battle, with the Antichrist and the ten kings sending their armies, led by fallen angels and demons, against Jerusalem (see Rev. 9:7–19; 16:14).

> A great people and a strong; there hath not been ever the like, neither shall be any more after it, even to the years of many generations. A fire devoureth before them; and behind them a flame burneth: the land is as the garden of Eden before them, and behind them a desolate wilderness; yea, and nothing shall escape them. The appearance of them is as the appearance of horses; and as horsemen, so shall they run. Like the noise of chariots on the tops of mountains shall they leap, like the noise of a flame of fire that devoureth the stubble, as a strong people set in battle array. Before their face the people shall be much pained: all faces shall gather blackness. They shall run like mighty men; they shall climb the wall like men of war; and they shall march every one on his ways, and they shall not break their ranks: Neither shall one thrust another; they shall walk every one in his path: and when they fall upon the sword, they shall not be wounded. They shall run to and fro in the city; they shall run upon the wall, they shall climb up upon the houses; they shall enter in at the windows like a thief. The earth shall quake before them; the heavens shall tremble: the sun and the moon shall be dark, and the stars shall withdraw their shining.
>
> —Joel 2:2–10

Then the Lord shall meet them on the battlefield with his great army from heaven.

> And the Lord shall utter his voice before his army: for his camp is very great: for he is strong that executeth his word: for the

day of the Lord is great and very terrible; and who can abide
it? . . . Let the priests, the ministers of the Lord, weep between
the porch and the altar, and let them say, Spare thy people, O
Lord, and give not thine heritage to reproach that the heathen
should rule over them: wherefore should they say among the
people, Where is their God? Then will the Lord be jealous for
his land and pity his people. Yea, the Lord will answer and say
unto his people, Behold, I will send you corn, and wine, and oil,
and ye shall be satisfied therewith: and I will no more make you
a reproach among the heathen. But I will remove far off from
you the northern army, and will drive him into a land barren
and desolate, with his face toward the east sea, and his hinder
part toward the utmost sea, and his stink shall come up, and
his ill savour shall come up, because he hath done great things.

—vv. 11, 17–20

The battle will rage throughout Jerusalem, outside the city, and
into the great valley until the armies of the nations are completely
annihilated. The Lord will also send a great plague, causing the
soldiers to turn their weapons on one another.

The Army of Antichrist

And this shall be the plague wherewith the Lord will smite
all the people that have fought against Jerusalem; Their flesh
shall consume away while they stand upon their feet, and
their eyes shall consume away in their holes, and their tongue
shall consume away in their mouth. And it shall come to pass
in that day, that a great tumult from the Lord shall be among
them; and they shall lay hold every one on the hand of his
neighbour, and his hand shall rise up against the hand of his
neighbour. . . . And so shall be the plague of the horse, of the
mule, of the camel, and of the ass, and of all the beasts that
shall be in these tents, as this plague.

—Zechariah 14:12–13, 15

And [the grapes in] the winepress were trodden outside the city, and blood poured from the winepress, [reaching] as high as the horses' bridles, for a distance of 1,600 stadia (about 200 miles).

—Revelation 14:20 (AMP)

Antichrist and the False Prophet

And the beast was seized and overpowered, and with him the false prophet who in his presence had worked wonders and performed miracles by which he led astray those who had accepted or permitted to be placed upon them the stamp (mark) of the beast and those who paid homage and gave divine honors to his statue. Both of them were hurled alive into the fiery lake that burns and blazes with brimstone.

—19:20 (AMP)

After the battle is over, the Bible tells us that all the birds will feed ravenously and glut themselves with the flesh of the defeated army. Then the Bible describes an angel who descends from heaven and lays hold of Satan.

Satan

And he gripped and overpowered the dragon, that old serpent [of primeval times], who is the devil and Satan, and [securely] bound him for a thousand years. Then he hurled him into the Abyss (the bottomless pit) and closed it and sealed it above him, so that he should no longer lead astray and deceive and seduce the nations until the thousand years were at an end. After that he must be liberated for a short time.

—20:2–3 (AMP)

A New Day on Earth

"But it shall come to pass that at evening time it shall be light" (Zech. 4:7). This Scripture promises that the darkness of that day will end and that the light of a new day will return to the earth. The day of the Lord's wrath will end, and the time of restoration will begin as the Lord commences his thousand-year reign on earth. The promise of the day of the Lord, given to King David in Psalm 2, has now been fulfilled.

> The kings of the earth set themselves, and the rulers take counsel together, against the Lord, and against his anointed, saying, Let us break their bands asunder, and cast away their cords from us. He that sitteth in the heavens shall laugh: the Lord shall have them in derision. Then shall he speak unto them in his wrath, and vex them in his sore displeasure. Yet have I set my king upon my holy hill of Zion. I will declare the decree: the Lord hath said unto me, Thou art my Son; this day have I begotten thee. Ask of me, and I shall give thee the heathen for thine inheritance, and the uttermost parts of the earth for thy possession.
>
> —vv. 2–8

When Jesus appeared to his disciples after his resurrection, they asked him, "Lord, is this the time when You will reestablish the kingdom and restore it to Israel?" (Acts 1:6 AMP). Jesus told them that it was not for them to know the times that were fixed by his Father, but now the day has come; it is the time when Jesus will restore the kingdom.

The next chapter is about restoring the kingdom to Israel and establishing the kingdom of God throughout the world. It will be a time of restitution, the greatest reconstruction the world has ever known. All creation has awaited this day "for we know that the whole creation groaneth and travaileth in pain together until now" (Rom. 8:22).

CHAPTER ELEVEN

Restoration

Repent ye therefore, and be converted, that your sins may be blotted out, when the times of refreshing shall come from the presence of the Lord. And he shall send Jesus Christ, which before was preached unto you: Whom heaven must receive until the times of restitution of all things, which God hath spoken by the mouth of all his holy prophets since the world began.

—Acts 3:19–21

THE KINGDOMS OF the world have now become the kingdom of our Lord. Every defiled thing of mankind has been shaken to its foundation, and a new world has come. Only the things that had their foundation in God could not be shaken and still remain. The kingdom will be restored like the garden of Eden with pleasant-looking plants and fragrant trees, which are good for food and watered by rivers and streams. Gold and precious stones will be abundant. Wildlife and mankind will dwell together in peace. In God's kingdom no one will be allowed to harm anything. The first order in the kingdom of God will be to restore nature to its original balance. From a hill in the center of the earth, the restoration will begin with a single drop of water.

THE ENVIRONMENT

The restoration will begin with water—clear, pure, holy water. The land surrounding Jerusalem will now be lifted up with the temple sitting high upon it. Living waters will begin to trickle and flow from under the altar of the temple. As the water flows from the high ground, half will flow toward the Mediterranean Sea, and half will flow the opposite direction to the Dead Sea. Wherever it flows, everything it touches will begin to live. The prophet Ezekiel experienced a vision of this restoration. In the vision an angel led him to trace its path.

> He measured a thousand cubits [566 yards], and he brought me through the waters; the waters were to the ankles. Again he measured a thousand, and brought me through the waters; the waters were to the knees. Again he measured a thousand, and brought me through; the waters were to the loins. Afterward he measured a thousand; and it was a river that I could not pass over: for the waters were risen, waters to swim in, a river that could not be passed over.
>
> —Ezekiel 47:3–5

After the angel took Ezekiel over a mile to explore the flow of the river, he brought him back by the same route; many trees were already growing on both sides at the river's bank. The angel showed him how the waters, which ran eastward, had entered the Dead Sea, which was now fresh and healed. Along its path across the desert wilderness, everything it touched had come to life. Many kinds of fish were in the sea, and there was no longer any salt in the sea, but the salt remained in its marshes. Fishermen were spreading their nets on its shores from Engedi to Eneglaim, two towns on the shore of the Dead Sea.

Then the angel showed Ezekiel the beauty and fragrance of the trees and the different fruits. He showed how the delightful fragrance of its fruits and leaves will bring health to the bones of the people as they flourish in good health and long life because the trees are fed by the holy, living waters (Isa. 66:14). "By the river on its bank, on one side and on the other, will grow all kinds of trees for food. Their leaves will not wither and their fruit will not fail. They will bear every month because their water flows from the sanctuary, and their fruit will be for food and their leaves for healing" (Ezek. 47:12 NASB).

BEULAH LAND

The angel then showed Ezekiel how the inheritance of the land was to be divided among the twelve tribes of Israel for their homes and possessions. The Lord's inheritance and the sanctuary were in the middle of it. Then the Lord gave both the people and the land new names. "And the Gentiles shall see thy righteousness, and all kings thy glory: and thou shalt be called by a new name, which the mouth of the Lord shall name. . . . Thou shalt no more be termed Forsaken; neither shall thy land any more be termed Desolate: but thou shalt be termed Hephzibah [My Delight], and thy land Beulah [Married]" (Isa. 62:2, 4 AMP).

The city of Jerusalem will also be called by another name—whether given by the Lord or by the people is unclear—which means "The Lord is there" (Ezek. 48:35). Based on the following Scripture in the book of Daniel that has been hard to understand, the restoration may possibly take only forty-five days. "And from the time that the continual burnt offering is taken away and the abomination that makes desolate is set up, there shall be 1290 days. Blessed, happy, fortunate, spiritually prosperous, and to be envied is he who waits expectantly and earnestly [who endures without wavering beyond the period of tribulation] and comes to the 1,335 days!" (Dan. 12:11–12 AMP).

The wilderness areas will spring to life, grass and trees will flourish, and rivers and streams in the desert will flow, causing the creatures of the wilderness to praise the Lord. The fragrance of trees, flowers, and herbs will fill the air. The desert will bloom with roses because of all the fresh springs and rivers. Isaiah also prophecies the following:

I will open rivers in high places, and fountains in the midst of the valleys: I will make the wilderness a pool of water, and the dry land springs of water. I will plant in the wilderness the cedar, the shittah [acacia] tree, and the myrtle, and the oil tree; I will set in the desert the fir tree, and the pine, and the box tree together: That they may see, and know, and consider, and understand together, that the hand of the Lord hath done this, and the Holy One of Israel hath created it.

—Isaiah 41:18–20

The animals and all wildlife will have a new nature and will no longer feed on one another. Instead they will eat straw and dwell together in peace (65:25), "And the suckling child shall play over the hole of the asp and the weaned child shall put his hand on the adder's den. They shall not hurt or destroy in all my holy mountain" (11:8–9 AMP).

NATIONS WILL FLOW TO BEULAH LAND

A great, glorious light will shine in Beulah Land, and all nations of the world will be drawn to it. Jerusalem will have no need of the sun to light the day nor the moon to light the night; the light of the Lord will outshine them both: "The sun shall be no more thy light by day; neither for brightness shall the moon give light unto thee: but the Lord shall be unto thee an everlasting light, and thy God thy glory. The sun shall no more go down; neither shall thy moon withdraw itself: for the Lord shall be thine everlasting light, and the days of thy mourning shall be ended" (Isa. 60:19–20).

The Gentile nations will see the light and the glory from afar. Just as those who weep at night rejoice when morning comes, so will the nations rejoice in this everlasting light in the city where there is no night, and they will be drawn to the place where the Lord dwells (v. 3). They will come bearing gold and incense and singing songs about Zion (v. 6). They will be drawn, not by their own human natures, but by the Holy Spirit. They will come to serve the Lord, to rebuild the land, and to minister before the Lord. Any nation that refuses and hardens their hearts against the drawing power of the Holy Spirit will waste away and perish from their own hardened hearts (v. 12). The gates of the city will not be shut day or night because of all those who come. "And the sons of strangers shall build up thy walls, and their kings shall minister unto thee. . . . Therefore thy gates shall be open continually; they shall not be shut day nor night; that men may bring unto thee the forces of the Gentiles, and that their kings may be brought" (vv. 10–11).

All of Hephzibah, the twelve tribes of Israel who are God's delight, shall become priests and ministers of God. The Lord will disperse some of them into other nations, where they will dwell, raise families, and be a light to the people. They will be like missionaries who return home from time to time. "But you shall be called the priests of the Lord; people will speak of you as the ministers of our God. You shall eat the wealth of the nations, and the glory [once that of your captors] shall be yours" (61:6 AMP).

These priests and ministers of the Lord will be recognized as those who are righteous and in a right standing with God. All the people will seek them out. "In those days it shall come to pass, that ten men shall take hold out of all languages of the nations, even shall take hold of the skirt of him that is a Jew, saying, We will go with you: for we have heard that God is with you" (Zech. 8:23).

The streets and park areas in Jerusalem will be full of joy, peace, and well-being as old men and women sit on benches with their canes while boys and girls play in the streets (vv. 4–5). The Lord will proclaim times of fasting in Judah as the condition for having love, truth, and peace. It will be a conditional promise of the Lord, and these will be times of joy and gladness many will look forward to and not disdain. Cheerful, appointed seasons of fasting will be observed in the fourth, fifth, seventh, and tenth months of the year (v. 19). People will come from afar to participate in these fasts as well as other events, and they will gather their friends and relatives to all go together. "It shall yet come to pass that there shall come [to Jerusalem] peoples and the inhabitants of many and great cities, And the inhabitants of

one city shall go to them of another, saying, Let us go speedily
to pray and entreat the favor of the Lord and to seek, inquire of,
and require [to meet our own most essential need] the Lord of
hosts. I will go also" (vv. 20–21 AMP).

TRADE AND COMMERCE

An interesting conversation took place between God and the
prophet Jeremiah roughly six hundred years before Christ was
born. Jeremiah had remained in Judah during the time most
Jews had been taken captive to Babylon. In Jeremiah 32:43–44,
God tells Jeremiah that even though Jeremiah said the land was
desolate without man or beast, and even though another nation
had conquered it, the day would come when "men shall buy fields
for money and shall sign deeds, seal them, and call witnesses
in the land of Benjamin, in the places around Jerusalem, in the
cities of Judah, in the cities of the hill country, in the cities of the
lowland, and in the cities of the South" (v. 44 AMP).

As the conversation continues in Jeremiah 32 and 33, it
becomes apparent that God is referring to a time in the distant
future when the Lord will reign and prosperity will be in the
land. He tells Jeremiah that at that time there will again be cities,
dwellings, pastures with flocks, and shepherds. The buying and
selling of flocks will also take place. God instructs Jeremiah to
buy a field in Anathoth in the land of Benjamin for seventeen
sheckles of silver. Jeremiah was to sign the deed before witnesses.
He was told to give the purchase deed to Baruch and charge him
to do the following according to the Word of God:

And I charged Baruch before them, saying, Thus says the Lord
of hosts, the God of Israel: Take these deeds, both this purchase
deed which is sealed and this unsealed deed, and put them in
an earthen vessel, that they may last a long time. For thus says
the Lord of hosts, the God of Israel: Houses and fields and
vineyards shall be purchased yet again in this land.

—Jeremiah 32:13–15 (AMP)

Jeremiah never recovered this deed in his lifetime. Shortly after this event, he left with a small group of the remaining Jews to Egypt, where he died. The question is, why did God instruct Jeremiah to do such a thing with the purchase deed, knowing that Jeremiah would die without enjoying the field he had purchased?

JEREMIAH'S INHERITANCE

Jeremiah will return to the land of Israel along with the Jews, whom God will keep safe during the tribulation period, but he will return in his resurrected body. The land he purchased approximately twenty-six hundred years before for seventeen shekels will probably be worth a fortune at that time. That is not to say that Jeremiah will want to sell it, but he will certainly be able to enjoy the fruits of a valuable field of land.

The point of this story is that it tells us something about life during the millennial reign of Christ. It tells us that everyday life will go on and that we who will have resurrected bodies will also participate in life on earth and enjoy its fruits in the kingdom of God.

HEALTH, SICKNESS, SIN, AND DEATH

As long as humans dwell on earth, there will be sin, sickness, and death. Even though Satan will be bound during this one-thousand-year period, evil spirits or demons will apparently remain, and death will not be destroyed until Christ's thousand-year reign ends and the great white throne judgment takes place (Rev. 18:2; 21:4). In spite of this fact, God's plan is for humans to live for a long time like the life of a tree, during this period.

There shall no more be in it an infant who lives but a few days, or an old man who dies prematurely; for the child shall die a hundred years old, and the sinner who dies when only a hundred years old shall be [thought only a child, cut off because he is] accursed. They shall build houses and inhabit them, and

they shall plant vineyards and eat the fruit of them. They shall
not build and another inhabit; they shall not plant and another
eat [the fruit]. For as the days of a tree, so shall be the days of
My people, and My chosen and elect shall long make use of
and enjoy the work of their hand.

—Isaiah 65:20–22 (AMP)

PRAYER

Communication with the Lord will be instantaneous no
matter where a person lives in the world. Whenever someone
cries out to God in prayer, the Lord will hear. Even before he or
she calls, God will know his or her need. He will immediately
respond with the answer through angels, resurrected saints,
or Jewish ministers. "And it shall be that before they call
I will answer; and while they are yet speaking I will hear"
(v. 24 AMP).

The world's inhabitants will experience what Christians have
experienced in their walk with the Lord as they have lived their
lives on this earth according to his Word concerning their prayers.
Jesus told them, "For your Father knows what you need before
you ask Him" (Matt. 6:8 AMP).

HUMAN NATURE

The resurrected saints will understand and recognize human
nature, and they will be aware that the flesh nature with its
lusts can become stronger than the spirit, even though Satan
is bound for one thousand years. Extrabiblical books like the
book of Jubilees and the book of Enoch indicate that evil spirits
or demons will remain on the earth to afflict and harass people
with God's permission (for chastisement) until the final judgment
day comes at the end of the millennial reign of Christ. These evil
spirits will be fully aware that God has allowed a certain time to
torment mankind. When Jesus cast out demons from two men,

the spirits questioned why he was doing this to them before the appointed time. "They shrieked and screamed, What have You to do with us, Jesus, Son of God? Have You come to torment us before the appointed time?" (Matt. 8:29 AMP). Evidently God will allow these evil spirits to remain as long as humans are on earth, but at the final judgment he will throw them into the lake of fire.

The next and final chapter will explore the role of the resurrected saints when they reign one thousand years with Christ.

CHAPTER TWELVE

The Saints

But the saints of the most High shall take the kingdom, and possess the kingdom for ever, even for ever and ever.

—Daniel 7:18

IN THE SERMON on the Mount, Jesus explicitly tells of those who will inherit the kingdom of God on earth. Those specifically mentioned include the poor in spirit, the meek, and those persecuted for the cause of righteousness. These are the primary traits of the saints, and the kingdom of God is their inheritance. We can see these traits tend to illustrate the forsaking of their own power and a turning to God's power. They have discovered that without Christ they can do nothing.

In their celestial bodies the saints will possess homes both in heaven and on earth. The kingdom of God will be simultaneously in heaven and on earth because the kingdom will be in Christ and in his saints. Wherever they rule, God will rule and the kingdom will exist. We also know that Christ will have a throne in heaven and on earth; his throne on earth will be in Jerusalem along with his twelve disciples. Jesus told the Twelve they would sit with him on thrones in Jerusalem and judge the twelve tribes of Israel (Matt. 19:28). To the other Christians he promises the following: "To him who overcomes, I will give the right to sit with me on my throne, just as I overcame and sat down with my Father on his throne" (Rev. 3:21 NIV).

Just as Christ will have a home in heaven and on earth, so also will the saints, for he promised them that where he is they would be also. "In my Father's house are many mansions: if it were not so, I would have told you. I go to prepare a place for you. And if I go and prepare a place for you, I will come again, and receive you unto myself; that where I am, there ye may be also" (John 14:2–3).

THE NATIONS

The survivors of the great tribulation will be those who refuse to take the mark of the beast or worship the image of the Antichrist. Scattered throughout the earth will be those who were out of the Antichrist's reach. Young children will not be required to take the mark, and for various reasons others will have no need to buy or sell. These will be the people who compose the Gentile nations of the world. They will be neither Christians nor Jews. They will be those who have not had judgment determined during their lifetimes.

The resurrected saints will serve as judges and rulers over certain areas of the Gentile world. Jesus told a parable about servants to whom their master gave his possessions to watch over while he was gone. When their master returned, he commented on how well each had done with the ten minas entrusted to them. Jesus was obviously referring to himself and his servants when he will return. "And he said to him, Well done, excellent bond servant! Because you have been faithful and trustworthy in a very little [thing], you shall have authority over ten cities. The second one also came and said, Lord, your mina has made five more minas. And he said also to him, And you will take charge over five cities" (Luke 19:17–19 AMP).

Another servant entrusted with his master's things took what he had been given and hid it instead of investing it. When the master returned and saw that it had produced nothing, he was angry and gave what otherwise would have been that servant's reward to others, who had been fruitful with what he gave to them. This is how the Lord will decide where and over how many cities his servants will rule.

THE REMAINING MANKIND

We may wonder about what kind of life surviving mortals will experience during this time. What kind of work will they do? Will they continue to marry and have families? We could ask other questions, but the answer to all of them is that mankind will behave as they always have, except nature and the world around them will be different. Children will do what children have always done; they will be active and play games. God showed the prophet Zechariah that children will play in Jerusalem's streets during the millennium (Zech. 8:5).

Their games will carry over to adulthood, and adults will remember the activities they loved before the tribulation period ended them. People need exercise and challenges, and many will possess various God-given talents they will use. They will labor because labor is ordained by God and will be necessary to tend and oversee the things God will give. Trees, gardens, animals, fish, and the various trades related to them will flourish. People will need farm equipment, kitchen utensils, and other necessary items in their communities. We know there will be fishermen because Ezekiel 47:10–11 tells us they will cast their nets in the Dead Sea. Sheep will need shearing, cows will need milking, cotton will be planted, clothes will be made, and music will fill the air.

THE SAINTS

The Bible doesn't provide any specifics of how or where the saints will actually live in their resurrected bodies. It doesn't tell us much about the joy and pleasures of the resurrected life for the saints other than the following promise from God: "For since the beginning of the world men have not heard, nor perceived by the ear, neither hath the eye seen, O God, beside thee, what he hath prepared for him that waiteth for him" (Isa. 64:4).

The Bible does, however, give us a great deal of information about how the saints will judge and rule in God's kingdom. First and foremost, the Bible tells us about Christ's rule, which will also apply to the saints.

> He shall judge thy people with righteousness, and thy poor with judgment. The mountains shall bring peace to the people, and the little hills, by righteousness. . . . He shall come down like rain upon the mown grass: as showers that water the earth. In his days shall the righteous flourish; and abundance of peace so long as the moon endureth. He shall have dominion also from sea to sea, and from the river unto the ends of the earth. . . . Yea, all kings shall fall down before him: all nations shall serve him. For he shall deliver the needy when he crieth; the poor also, and him that hath no helper. He shall spare the poor and needy, and shall save the souls of the needy. He shall redeem their soul from deceit and violence: and precious shall their blood be in his sight. And he shall live, and to him shall be given the gold of Sheba: prayer also shall be made for him continually; and daily shall he be praised.
>
> —Psalm 72:2–3, 6–8, 11–15

Christ will rule over the entire world, and Scripture indicates that resurrected King David will rule over Beulah Land (Israel) under Christ. "But they shall serve the Lord their God, and David their king, whom I will raise up unto them" (Jer. 30:9).

The saints will judge and rule under the authority of Christ, much like appointed judges helped Moses rule over and judge the great multitude of people in the wilderness when they were coming to him from morning to evening. His father-in-law asked him why he was doing this task alone. "And Moses said unto his father in law, Because the people come unto me to inquire of God: When they have a matter, they come unto me; and I judge between one and another, and I do make them know the statutes of God, and his laws" (Ex. 18:15–16).

The books of Deuteronomy and 2 Samuel also provide guidelines for how God expects us to judge.

> Judges and officers shalt thou make thee in all thy gates, which the Lord thy God giveth thee, throughout thy tribes: and they shall judge the people with just judgment. Thou shalt not wrest judgment; thou shalt not respect persons, neither take a gift: for a gift doth blind the eyes of the wise, and pervert the words of the righteous.
>
> —Deuteronomy 16:18–19

> He that ruleth over men must be just, ruling in the fear of God. And he shall be as the light of the morning, when the sun riseth, even a morning without clouds; as the tender grass springing out of the earth by clear shining after rain.
>
> —2 Samuel 23:3–4

Laws will go forth from the Lord to regulate life in the communities with justice and righteousness, and the saints will administer those laws.

> And he will teach us of his ways, and we will walk in his paths: for out of Zion *shall go forth the law*, and the word of the Lord from Jerusalem. And he shall judge among the nations, and shall rebuke many people: and they shall beat their swords into plowshares, and their spears into pruning hooks: nation shall not lift up sword against nation, neither shall they learn war any more.
>
> —Isaiah 2:3–4 (emphasis mine)

This administration of law will be a new covenant, which will be different from the law God gave through Moses. The prophet Jeremiah foretold this.

> Behold, the days come, saith the Lord, that I will make a new covenant with the house of Israel, and with the house of Judah:

Not according to the covenant that I made with their fathers in the day that I took them by the hand to bring them out of the land of Egypt; which my covenant they brake, although I was an husband unto them saith thee Lord: But this shall be the covenant that I will make with the house of Israel; After those days, saith the Lord, I will put my law in their inward parts, and write it in their hearts; and will be their God, and they shall be my people. And they shall teach no more every man his neighbour, and every man his brother, saying, Know the Lord: for they shall all know me, from the least of them unto the greatest of them, saith the Lord: for I will forgive their iniquity, and I will remember their sin no more.

—Jeremiah 31:31–34

Hebrews 10:1 tells us that the first law "was merely a rude outline (foreshadowing) of the good things to come—instead of fully expressing those things" (AMP). The new covenant with Israel will be a mixture of grace and law; grace will open the door for them to know the Lord, and the law will help them walk in his ways. This spirit of grace will be poured out on the nation of Israel on the day of the Lord, when they will repent as they recognize Jesus as the rejected Messiah. "And I will pour upon the house of David, and upon the inhabitants of Jerusalem, the spirit of grace and of supplications: and they shall look upon me whom they have pierced, and they shall mourn for him, as one mourneth for his only son, and shall be in bitterness for him, as one that is in bitterness for his firstborn" (Zech. 12:10).

The inhabitants of the world will live under the law. The law will be swiftly and strictly enforced so evil, unrighteousness, and war do not gain a foothold in the world. The saints will rule with a rod of iron, just as Jesus will rule with a rod of iron to protect the people from harm.

And he that overcometh, and keepeth my works unto the end, to him will I give power over the nations: And he shall rule them with a rod of iron; as the vessels of a potter shall they be broken to shivers: even as I received of my Father. And I will give him the morning star.

—Revelation 2:26–28

Nation shall not lift up a sword against nation, neither shall they learn war any more.

—Micah 4:3

FAITH, HOPE, AND LOVE

All spiritual gifts imparted by the Holy Spirit—those that give a partial knowledge of God, such as prophecy, tongues, and knowledge—will be done away with because we will no longer only know in part. We will be fully known and fully know. What will not be done away with is faith, hope, and love. And the law will be administered and obeyed with these three spiritual attributes among the judges and rulers.

But where there are prophecies, they will cease; where there are tongues, they will be stilled; where there is knowledge, it will pass away. For we know in part and we prophesy in part, but when perfection comes, the imperfect disappears. . . . Now we see but a poor reflection as in a mirror; then we shall see face to face. Now I know in part; then I shall know fully, even as I am fully known. And now these three remain: faith, hope and love. But the greatest of these is love.

—1 Corinthians 13:8–10, 12–13 (NIV)

For the earth will be full of the knowledge of the Lord As the waters cover the sea.

—Isaiah 11:9 (NASB)

The age of grace for the Gentile nations was a great parenthetical period ordained by God to gather the rest of the world into the same plan he had for the nation of Israel, Abraham's descendants. Now that the parentheses are closed, God will return to his plan for Israel and the Messiah, who will rule the world from Jerusalem as King and Priest.

THE FEAST OF TABERNACLES

The Jews will celebrate the Feast of Tabernacles each year as they always have, and the people in other nations will also go up to Jerusalem to worship Christ at this time every year.

> And everyone who is left of all the nations which came against Jerusalem shall even go up from year to year to worship the King, the Lord of hosts, and to keep the Feast of Tabernacles or Booths. And it shall be that whoso of the families of the earth shall not go up to Jerusalem to worship the King, the Lord of hosts, upon them there shall be no rain.
>
> —Zechariah 14:16–17 (AMP)

God gave the nation of Israel this feast as a holy convocation and a statute to be celebrated forever throughout all their generations. It is held every year, beginning on the fifteenth day of the seventh month in the Jewish religious calendar. Held at the beginning of autumn, it corresponds to September in our calendar and coincides with the final harvesting of the crops of the land. God told Moses to do the following during this celebration: "Ye shall dwell in booths seven days; all that are Israelites born shall dwell in booths: That your generations may know that I made the children of Israel to dwell in booths, when I brought them out of the land of Egypt" (Lev. 23:42–43).

The feast is a joyous time and a time for celebration. What a week! Just envision that the twelve disciples and all Old Testament saints, including Abraham, Isaac, Jacob, Moses, Elijah and King David, will be there. Everyone in the great hall of faith will be there. One can only imagine the wonderful testimonies all these saints will give, even more than the Word of God could contain. What a time of fellowship and singing! Knowledge about heaven will greatly increase as the Lord and the resurrected saints will testify about it. Even the half cannot be told or even imagined because "Eye hath not seen, nor ear heard, neither have entered into the heart of man, the things which God hath prepared for them that love him" (1 Cor. 2:9).

In the following epilogue, we will discuss what will happen at the end of the thousand-year reign of Christ and the saints as well as the glory of our final destination—heaven.

Epilogue

AS WONDERFUL AS the millennial reign of Christ will be, its ending is hard to understand unless we truly understand Satan's deceptive power. We should be able to understand it simply by looking at the world around us and our own life experience. When we see the evil and cruelty in the world, and when we see the people we know follow a path leading only to destruction, yet refuse to change and avoid it, we recognize deception.

If we truly understood the deception in our society today, then we could begin to understand what will happen when the thousand years come to an end. Even if we could understand the ending, we would probably be powerless to stop it. Something strong in mankind compels us to obey the lusts of our flesh and the pride of our lives. If someone in authority intervenes to curtail those destructive impulses, that authority becomes a hated enemy, and rebellion follows.

Though Satan will be bound for one thousand years, nothing in the Bible tells us that the evil spirits or demons will be bound as well. In fact, it appears they will be allowed to harass, trouble, afflict, and torment mankind until the day of the great judgment.[17] When the thousand years are over, the following will take place:

> "And when the thousand years are expired, Satan shall be loosed out of his prison, And shall go out to deceive the nations which are in the four quarters of the earth, Gog, and Magog,

to gather them together to battle: the number of whom is as the sand of the sea. And they went up on the breadth of the earth, and compassed the camp of the saints about, and the beloved city: and fire came down from God out of heaven, and devoured them."

—Revelation 20:7–9

Fire will devour all who are deceived by Satan, and he will be cast into the fire and brimstone of hell, to be tormented day and night forever and ever. The battle of the ages is finally over! Jesus will then deliver the kingdom to the Father.

After that comes the end (the completion), when He delivers over the kingdom to God the Father after rendering inoperative and abolishing every [other] rule and every authority and power. For [Christ] must be King and reign until He has put all [His] enemies under His feet. The last enemy to be subdued and abolished is death.

—1 Corinthians 15:24–26 (AMP)

THE GREAT WHITE THRONE JUDGMENT

Immediately after God throws Satan into the lake of fire, the remainder of the dead—all who ever lived on earth and were not raised in the first resurrection—will be raised from the dead. The apostle John saw all of these people stood before the throne in heaven. He also saw this present heaven and earth had fled away, never to be found again, at the appearing of God on his throne. The prophet Daniel also saw a vision of God on the day of judgment and describes the vision as follows:

I kept looking until thrones were placed [for the assessors with the Judge], and the Ancient of Days [God, the eternal Father] took His seat, Whose garment was white as snow and the hair of His head like pure wool. His throne was like the fiery flame; its wheels were burning fire. A stream of fire came forth from before Him; a thousand thousands ministered to Him and ten thousand times ten thousand rose up and stood before Him; the Judge was seated [the court was in session] and the books were opened.

—Daniel 7:9–10 (AMP)

The apostle Peter speaks of this day as the "day of God" (2 Peter 3:12) because it will be the day of the last judgment. The first judgment on the world, other than God's judgment in Noah's day, will be the day of God's wrath on the nations of the earth. This last judgment will be on all individuals who have ever been born. Romans 14:10 says, "For we will all stand before the judgment seat of God" (NASB). Peter describes what will become of this present earth and heaven on the great judgment day as follows:

But the day of the Lord will come like a thief, and then the heavens will vanish (pass away) with a thunderous crash, and the [material] elements [of the universe] will be dissolved with fire, and the earth and the works that are upon it will be burned up. . . . What kind of person ought [each of] you to be [in the meanwhile] in consecrated and holy behavior and devout and godly qualities, While you wait and earnestly long for (expect and hasten) the coming of the day of God by reason of which the flaming heavens will be dissolved, and the [material] elements [of the universe] will flare and melt with fire?

—2 Peter 3:10–12 (AMP)

Immediately after the great white throne judgment, the apostle John saw what Peter described.

And I saw a new heaven and a new earth: for the first heaven and the first earth had passed away; and there was no more sea. And I John saw the holy city, new Jerusalem, coming down from God out of heaven, prepared as a bride adorned for her husband. And I heard a great voice out of heaven saying, "Behold, the tabernacle of God is with men, and he will dwell with them, and they shall be his people, and God himself shall be with them, and be their God."

—Revelation 21:1–3

The Bible tells us that all who have lived and died will stand before the judgment seat of God. Hebrews 9:27 says, "It is appointed for [all] men once to die, and after this the [certain] judgment" (AMP). At this judgment John saw that books were opened. We do not know how many books will be opened; we know only that there will be more than one book. Then John saw that there was another book opened beside them. It is the Book of Life.

THE BOOK OF LIFE

The Bible mentions this Book of Life many times. No references indicate that events are written in it as we progress through our lives or that our names are written in it at the moment we accept Christ as our Savior. To the contrary, every indication is that God's plan for our lives—his purpose from our births—was already written in this book before the foundation of the world. Furthermore, every indication is that men and women can be erased or blotted out of the Book of Life. This book is also sometimes referred to as the Lamb's Book of Life because all God's plans are in Christ, and only through him can they be fulfilled.

Moses made the first mention of the Book of Life in the Bible when those he was shepherding in the wilderness sinned by making an idol of gold. Moses recognized what a great sin this was to the God who had redeemed them, and he feared that God might erase their names from the Book of Life. He interceded with God for them, even to the point of offering himself for their sin. Here is how Moses pleaded: "Yet now, if You will forgive their sin—and if not, blot me, I pray You, out of Your book which You have written! But the Lord said to Moses, Whoever has sinned against Me, I will blot him [not you] out of My book" (Ex. 32:32–33 AMP). The

Lord heeded this intercessory prayer of Moses and did not blot the people out of the Book of Life. Nevertheless, he punished the people for their sins by sending a plague upon them.

Righteous Job in the midst of his suffering pleaded with God and spoke many words, which became testimonies of his suffering and his faith. Then one day he spoke these prophetic words: "Oh, that the words I now speak were written! Oh, that they were inscribed in a book" (Job 19:23 AMP).

We know that the words *were* inscribed in a book. Even though Job didn't know it at the time he spoke these words, he later came to believe that his suffering was in God's plan for his life, the plan written in the Book of Life for him, because he later proclaims, "For He performs [that which He has] planned for me, and of many such matters He is mindful" (23:14 AMP).

King David experienced a similar suffering when he was troubled on all sides by enemies who wanted to trample him. He wrote the following, expressing his faith in God and his plan for him: "You number and record my wanderings; put my tears into Your bottle—are they not in Your book?" (Ps. 56:8 AMP).

David also wrote the following when he understood that God knew everything ordained for him: "Your eyes saw my unformed substance, and in Your book all the days [of my life] were written before ever they took shape, when as yet there was none of them" (139:16 AMP).

The book of Hebrews quotes from a prophecy about Christ in Psalm 40:6–8, which speaks of Christ being born into this world to perform the things ordained for him. In it Christ declares what the Book of Life is all about when he says the following: "In burnt offerings and sin offerings You have taken no delight. Then I said, Behold, here I am, coming to do Your will, O God—[to fulfill] what is written of Me in the volume of the Book" (Heb. 10:6–7 AMP).

The book of Revelation contains references about being erased from the Book of Life, which was written from the foundation of the world, as follows:

Thus shall he who conquers (is victorious) be clad in white garments, and I will not erase or blot out his name from the Book of Life; I will acknowledge him [as Mine] and I will confess his name openly before My Father and before His angels.

—Revelation 3:5 (AMP)

And if any man shall take away from the words of the book of this prophecy, God shall take away his part out of the book of life, and out of the holy city, and from the things which are written in this book.

—22:19

In reference to the New Jerusalem that will descend from heaven, John describes who will and who will not enter into it as only those written in the Lamb's Book of Life: "And there shall in no wise enter into it any thing that defileth, neither whatsoever worketh abomination, or maketh a lie: but they which are written in the Lamb's book of life" (21:27).

THE SECOND DEATH

Revelation 20:6 says, "Blessed and holy is he that hath part in the first resurrection: on such the second death hath no power." The questions then are these: What about all those who didn't have part in the first resurrection? Are they all lost and doomed? Some say this judgment will not be a trial but a time of sentencing. If that is true, then all who did not take part in the first resurrection have already been judged to be wicked. Some say that if these resurrected dead have not accepted Christ as their Savior, they will not be in the Book of Life and will therefore be doomed. Is this true?

Let me say before we examine these questions that I do not know the answers, but I surely do know the questions. I have heard them all my life. Here are some examples: What about those in unreachable areas of the world who have never heard of Jesus or the gospel? What about the Jewish people who still worship God? What about those killed in early adulthood who didn't have a chance to make a decision? What about those who believe in God and Christ but are ignorant of the requirements of the gospel? What about those who will go into the millennium or will be born during it? They will be in the last resurrection. Will they be lost, or will they be in the Book of Life?

Though I do not know the answers to these questions, I have searched for them. I will tell you what I have discovered during my lifetime. First and foremost, I know that God doesn't wish anyone to perish. During the three days when Jesus was buried in the earth, he descended in the spirit to the lower parts of the earth "in which He went and preached to the spirits in prison (The souls of those) who long before in the days of Noah had been disobedient" (1 Pet. 3:19–20 AMP). Ephesians 4:8–10 also explains "ascended" and "descended" as follows: "Wherefore he saith, When he ascended on high, he led captivity captive, and gave gifts unto men. (Now that he ascended, what is it but that he also descended first into the lower parts of the earth? He that descended is the same also that ascended up far above all heavens, that he might fill all things.)"

I have always understood these Scriptures to mean that Jesus descended into Sheol to preach and then took those dead in Sheol (the place of all the departed dead before Paradise was opened for the righteous in heaven with Jesus), who had been disobedient during the days of Noah, with him to Paradise when he ascended. God is ever mindful of those who have not received the gospel. Even after the rapture and resurrection, God will send three angels to preach the gospel in "midheaven," telling all mankind to worship God and warning them not to worship Antichrist or to take his mark, for all who do so will be tormented with fire and brimstone (Rev. 14:9–10).

I know that in the Jewish Talmud (a collection of ancient Jewish writings constituting religious authority in Orthodox Judaism) and in their celebration of the Feast of Tabernacles, the Jews teach that God possesses three books: the book of those who have been judged wicked, the book of those who have been judged righteous, and an intermediate book for those God did not judge in their lifetimes as being either wicked or righteous.

I know that Enoch in the book of Enoch claimed that he was shown three hollow places in Sheol: one that contained the souls of sinners who were "complete in their transgressions," one "for the righteous," and one "for those who were sinners during their lifetimes but judgment had not been executed when they died" (Book of Enoch XXII: 9). Enoch also saw that Abel, whom Cain had slain, was in that place (Book of Enoch XXII: 7);[18] and the Bible tells us that Cain's works were evil but that Abel's works were righteous (1 John 3:12). I can only surmise that Abel didn't have the opportunity to live out his full lifetime in order to know how he would be judged.

The apostle Paul knew that at least some of the Jewish people were being baptized for the dead, apparently in the hope of their salvation. He didn't take the opportunity to approve or rebuke them for this baptism but simply used it to show that without the resurrection we have no hope. He said the following: "Else what shall they do which are baptized for the dead, if the dead rise not at all? why are they then baptized for the dead?" (1 Cor. 15:29). The question is, will it be a resurrection of life or a resurrection of damnation (John 5:29)?

I realize that God ignored many things people did out of ignorance. Even the apostle Paul says, "Though I formerly blasphemed and persecuted and was shamefully and outrageously and aggressively insulting [to Him], nevertheless, I obtained mercy because I had acted out of ignorance in unbelief" (1 Tim. 1:13 AMP). Acts 17:29–30 tells us that in times past men made idols to worship, but because they did so in ignorance, God ignored their behavior and allowed it to pass unnoticed. The apostle Paul writes in Rom. 4:15 that "the Law results in [divine] wrath, but where there is no law there is no transgression [of it either]" (AMP).

I know that whosoever believes in Jesus will not perish but will have eternal life (John 3:16). I also know that no man can come to Jesus unless God the Father draws him and that every man who has heard and learned of God the Father comes to Jesus

(6:44–45). Psalm 9:10 promises that God will not forsake anyone who truly seeks him.

I also know that these resurrected dead will be judged by their works, which are found written in the books. It seems implied that their names might still be found in the Book of Life. Revelation 20:15, specifically says, "*If* their names are not found in the Book of Life they will be thrown into the lake of fire." Could this mean that some names might not have been erased or blotted out of the Book of Life?

> I [also] saw the dead, great and small; they stood before the throne, and books were opened. Then another book was opened, which is [the Book] of Life. And the dead were judged (sentenced) by what they had done [their whole way of feeling and acting, their aims and endeavors] in accordance with what was recorded in the books. And the sea delivered up the dead who were in it, death and Hades (the state of death or disembodied existence) surrendered the dead in them, and all were tried and their cases determined by what they had done [according to their motives, aims, and works]. Then death and Hades (the state of death or disembodied existence) were thrown into the lake of fire. This is the second death, the lake of fire. And if anyone's [name] was not found recorded in the Book of Life, he was hurled into the lake of fire.
>
> —Revelation 20:12–15 (AMP)

I know that God will judge both the righteous and the wicked with his truth and that men and women will give an account of every idle word they have spoken. By their words they will be justified or condemned. Every secret deed will be brought to light, whether good or evil. All will be revealed, and their works will be tried by fire. Those works the fire does not burn up will remain.

Finally, I know that God alone knows the counsels of the heart and will examine every work by its motives and aims. That is why no one can judge these people. As much as we may know, we can never know what God knows.

However, we do know that those who are judged to be wicked and unbelieving, who have never repented of the following sins, will have their part in the lake of fire. "But the fearful, and unbelieving, and the abominable, and murderers, and whoremongers, and sorcerers, and idolaters, and all liars, shall have their part in the lake which burneth with fire and brimstone: which is the second death" (21:8).

HEAVEN

When this present heaven and earth melt with fervent heat, a new heaven and a new earth will appear, but there will no longer be any sea. The holy city, called New Jerusalem, will descend from heaven, and God's home will be with men. This is heaven! Many believe that this present heaven and earth have always been just an image or shadow of the real heaven and earth. The Bible seems to confirm this. Hebrews 8:5 tells us that those on earth who serve in the temple "serve unto the example and shadow of the heavenly things." On the mountain God told Moses to make everything according to the pattern he had been given (because it was a copy of the heavenly).

In Chapters XXV–XXXVI in the extra-biblical book of Enoch, Enoch describes the holy angels of heaven taking him on a journey. There he saw great mountains, streams of water, clouds and dew, valleys and lakes, varied and attractive animals and birds, different plants, and aromatic and colorful trees such as the cinnamon, frankincense and myrrh.

Hebrews 12 speaks about a great cloud of witnesses and a New Jerusalem. The apostle Paul tells the Jewish Christians that they have not come to a burning mountain that cannot be touched as in the day of Moses. "But ye are come unto mount Sion, and unto the city of the living God, the heavenly Jerusalem, and to an innumerable company of angels" (v. 22).

If all this is true, this present earth is just a passing, temporal image of what has its eternal reality in heaven and is resplendent in glory. The Bible has not given a description of the new heaven and new earth, but we do have a description of the great city (New Jerusalem) where God dwells. The millennial reign of Christ will restore this present earth to the original Eden, but it will pass away because, being only an image, it cannot compare to the reality of the new earth.

Referring to the third heaven, the apostle Paul wrote in AD 55 that fourteen years earlier he had been caught up into paradise, where he heard unspeakable words (2 Cor. 12:2–4). Writing about heaven, he says, "Since we consider and look not to the things that are seen but to the things that are unseen; for the things that are visible are temporal (brief and fleeting), but the things that are invisible are deathless and everlasting" (2 Cor. 4:18 AMP). The following description of the New Jerusalem in Revelation 21:10–23 and 22:1–2 reveals the magnified beauty and greatness of what has its true existence in heaven:

1. The New Jerusalem will resemble a rare and precious jewel like jasper, clear and sparkling as crystal.

2. The city will have a high and massive wall with twelve gates around it. Each of the twelve gates will be built out of one solid, beautiful pearl. On the twelve gates will be the names of the twelve tribes of Israel.

3. The city's wall will feature twelve foundation stones to support the massive wall. The names of the twelve apostles of Jesus will be written on the twelve foundation stones. Each of the twelve foundation stones will be made of one of the following precious stones in the following order:

    1. Jasper
    2. Sapphire
    3. Chalcedony (white agate)
    4. Emerald
    5. Onyx

6. Sardius
7. Chrysolite
8. Beryl
9. Topaz
10. Chrysoprase
11. Jacinth
12. Amethyst

4. New Jerusalem will be fifteen hundred miles long, fifteen hundred miles wide, and fifteen hundred miles high. Its walls will be seventy-two yards thick, and the wall above the foundation stones will be made of pure jasper.

5. The city will be all pure gold, clear and transparent like clear glass. The main street running through the city will also be pure gold and translucent like opaque glass.

6. No temple will be in the city because God himself will be the temple. There will no longer be any need for the sun or the moon because God will be the light, and the Christ will be the lamp.

7. A river, sparkling like crystal, will flow from the throne of God and the Lamb.

8. The tree of life is on either side of the river, bearing twelve different fruits and the leaves will be for healing.

Blessed are they that do his commandments,
that they may have right to the tree of life,
and may enter in through the gates into the city.

—Revelation 22:14

Amen.

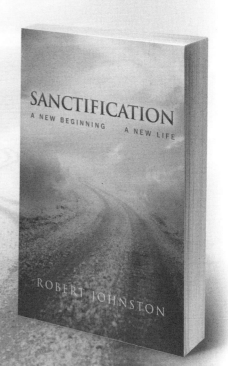

Endnotes

1. *Zondervan Pictorial Encyclopedia of the Bible*, Merrill C. Tenney,Volume A–C, "Aeon," F. Folkes, (Grand Rapids, MI. Zondervan, 1975, 1976), 67.

2. R. H. Charles, "Introduction," *The Book of Enoch or I Enoch*, 2009 Edition (Muskogee, OK. Artisan Publishers, 2004), 7.

3. *Zondervan Pictorial Encyclopedia of the Bible*, Merrill C. Tenney,Volume D–G, "Ephesus," E.M. Blaiklock, (Grand Rapids, MI. Zondervan, 1975, 1976), 324–332.

4. *Zondervan Pictorial Encyclopedia of the Bible*, Merrill C. Tenney,Volume Q–Z, "Smyrna," E.M. Blaiklock, (Grand Rapids, MI. Zondervan, 1975,1976), 462–464.

5. *Zondervan Pictorial Encyclopedia of the Bible*, Merrill C. Tenney, Volume M–P, "Pergamum," E.M. Blaiklock, (Grand Rapids, MI. Zondervan 1975,1976) 702.

6. *Zondervan Pictorial Encyclopedia of the Bible*, Merrill C. Tenney, Volume Q–Z, "Thyatra," W.M. Ramsay, E.M. Blaiklock, (Grand Rapids, MI. Zondervan, 1975,1976),743–744.

7. *Zondervan Pictorial Encyclopedia of the Bible*, Merrill C. Tenney, Volume Q–Z,"Sardis," E.M. Blaiklock, (Grand Rapids, MI. Zondervan, 1975,1976), 276–278.

8. *Zondervan Pictorial Encyclopedia of the Bible,* Merrill C. Tenney, Volume M–P, "Philadelphia," E.M. Blaiklock, (Grand Rapids, MI. Zondervan 1975,1976) 753.

9. *Zondervan Pictorial Encyclopedia of the Bible,* Merrill C. Tenney, Volume H–L, "Laodicea," W. White, Jr. (Grand Rapids, MI. Zondervan, 1975, 1976), 878–879.

10. The New International Webster's Collegiate Dictionary of the English Language International Encyclopedic Edition, 2002, Trident Press International, 346,414,661.

11. "United Church of Christ," AbsoluteAstronomy.com, http://www.absoluteastronomy.com/topics/United_Church_of_Christ. Pg. 1, 11/29/09.

12. United Church of Christ And Homosexuality, UCC Statements of Inclusivily. http://religioustolerance.org/hom_uccal.htm. Pg. 1, 11/25/09.

13. B. A. Robinson, "Liberal-Conservative Divisions within the Episcopal Church," ReligiousTolerance.org, Ontario Consultants on Religious Tolerance, last modified September 24, 2000, http://www.religioustolerance.org/div_epis.htm. Pg. 1, 11/25/09.

14. B. A. Robinson, "The Episcopal Church, USA and homosexuality," ReligiousTolerance.org, Ontario Consultants on Religious Tolerance, last modified September 22, 2007, http://www.religioustolerance.org/hom_epis.htm.

15. Jane Bingham, Fiona Chandler, and Sam Taplin, *The Usborne Internet-Linked Encyclopedia of the Roman World* (Tulsa, OK. E.D.C. Publishing, 2002), 41.

16. Philip Schaff, *History of the Christian Church*, vol. 2 (Grand Rapids, MI. Wm. B. Eerdman's Publishing Company, 1975, 1976), 75.

17. R.H. Charles, *The Book of Enoch or 1 Enoch*, 2009 Edition (Muskogee, OK. Artisian Publishers, 2004) XVI.1, 37.

18. R.H. Charles, *The Book of Enoch or I Enoch*, 2009 Edition (Muskogee, OK. Artisian Publishers, 2004).

Helps

For Understanding These Prophecies

The prophet Ezekiel was a captive in Babylon almost 600 years before Christ was born, when God began giving him visions and prophecies. The Amplified Bible's introduction to the Book of Ezekiel summarizes the essence of Ezekiel's visions and prophecies about the last days as follows:

> After the news reached Babylon that Jerusalem actually had been destroyed in 586 BC Ezekiel proclaimed a new message of hope and restoration. God as the great Shepherd will regather the Israelites from the ends of the earth and reestablish them in their own land. The nations who challenge Israel's return will be defeated and judged.

Ezekiel 37 prophesies of the regathering of the Jewish people out of all the nations in the world to reestablish them in their homeland of Israel. This regathering began in 1947 and is continuing today. God also told Ezekiel that the sanctuary and tabernacle will once again be built and God will renew his covenant with them. Chapters 38–39 describe the invasion of Islamic forces that will descend upon Israel to wipe them out and how God alone will supernaturally defend Israel and destroy all the invading forces with rain, pestilence, hailstones, fire and brimstone. Chapters 40–42 give detailed instructions for the construction of the Temple they will once again build in Jerusalem and describes how they will again offer sacrifices. Chapters 43–46 describe the glory of the Lord filling the Temple when he returns to earth at the end of the tribulation period. Chapter 47 describes how the world will be renewed and restored after the great destruction of the tribulation and the wrath of God. Chapter 48 gives the dimensions of earthly Jerusalem and the territory assigned to the twelve tribes of Israel with their gates. It is interesting that earthly Jerusalem is laid out in the same pattern as heavenly Jerusalem except the dimensions are much smaller.

People want to know what to watch for and what signs will tell us that the last days are coming upon us. The greatest sign, I believe, which cannot be missed by anyone, saved or unsaved, is the invasion of Israel by Islamic forces as predicted in Ezekiel 38. God, when describing his supernatural intervention to save his people, states, *"And I will make My holy name known in the midst of My people Israel, and I will not let them profane My holy name any more: and the nations shall know, understand, and realize that I am the Lord, the Holy One of Israel"* (Ezek. 39:7, AMP). Sometime after the destruction of the Islamic armies the leaders from many nations, (including one who will become known as the Antichrist), will sign a seven year covenant with the nation of Israel which will allow them to rebuild their Temple in peace.

This peace covenant will signal the start of the seven year tribulation period. The following timeline will help in understanding the order of tribulation and post tribulation events.

—Robert Johnston

Contents

For Prophetic Timeline of Future Events

Prophetic Timeline of Future Events

Pre-Tribulation Events

- **A political leader** (Antichrist) will arise in Europe who will unite the nations and bring peace and stability to the region (Dan. 8:25; 11:21, 24).

- **A great army** from Islamic nations will invade Israel from the North. All nations will abandon Israel leaving that nation defenseless against the overwhelming number of invaders. God alone will defend Israel, sending pestilence, torrents of rain, fire, and brimstone on the invaders, causing them to turn their weapons on one another. All nations will know that it is Israel's God who has saved them (Ezek. 38 and 39 AMP).

- **Many nations** will confirm a seven-year peace covenant with Israel, allowing it to rebuild its temple in peace and to offer sacrifices on the altar. One of the signers of the covenant will be Antichrist, known as a "man of peace." The covenant will signal the start of the seven-year tribulation period (Dan. 9:27).

Unless noted as "AMP" for *Amplified Bible Version* of the Bible, all verses are taken from the *King James Version* (KJV).

First Half of the Tribulation—First Five Seals—
"The Early Pains"

YEAR ONE—FIRST THREE SEALS

- **Antichrist** will be crowned king (Rev. 6:2).

- **Jews will rebuild** their temple in Jerusalem and offer sacrifices (Ezek. 40–46; Dan. 8:11).

- **Two witnesses** will begin their three-and-one-half years (1,260 days) of prophesying in Jerusalem (Rev. 11:3).

- **There will be wars** and rumors of wars (Rev. 6:4; Matt. 24:6).

- **There will be earthquakes,** food shortages, and inflation (Matt. 24:7; Rev. 6:5–7).

YEAR TWO—FOURTH SEAL

- **Propaganda attacks** will bring hatred and persecution of Christians (Matt. 24:9–10).

- **Many will fall** from the faith (2 Thess. 2:3).

- **Famine, violence,** and wild beasts will kill one-fourth of the world's population (Rev. 6:8).

Year Three—Fifth Seal

- **Hatred of Christians** will bring accusations, arrests, and trials that will be broadcast "unto all nations" (Matt. 24:14). The Holy Spirit will give the saints words to speak at these trials (Mark 13:12–13; Luke 21:12–14; Rev. 6:9). All listeners will hear in their own language and dialect (Acts 2:8, 16–21 AMP).

- **The Holy Spirit's** words will convert many hearts to God as the trials progress (Matt. 24:14; Mark 13:9–11; Acts 2:21; Dan. 7:26). This will alarm and enrage Antichrist.

- **Preaching the gospel** will be forbidden bringing a famine of hearing the word of the Lord (Amos 8:11–12, John 9:4). In Jerusalem many will try to kill the two witnesses to stop their prophesying, but fire will proceed from their mouths, consuming their adversaries (Rev. 11:5).

Midpoint of Tribulation—The Sixth Seal—
"The Rapture"

YEAR FOUR—VICTORY AND DELIVERANCE

- **Testimonies of the saints** at their trials will invade the kingdom of Antichrist (Dan. 7:26 AMP). Antichrist will abruptly and hastily order his armies to surround Jerusalem and stop the sacrifices (Dan. 7:26 AMP).

- **God will pass** righteous judgment in favor of the saints against the accuser (Dan. 7:22, 25–26 AMP), bringing war in heaven (Rev. 12:7). Satan and his angels will be cast out of the first (lowest) heaven (Eph. 2:2; 6:12 AMP; John 12:31 AMP) and down to earth by God's angels, bringing Satan's wrath to people on earth (Rev. 12:8–11 AMP).

- **Antichrist will enter** the Temple in Jerusalem and announce he is God (2 Thess. 2:4 AMP), and then declare war on Jews and Christians (Rev. 12:13,17 AMP; Dan. 9:27 AMP).

- **The Jews will flee** to a place of safety where they will be fed and protected by God for the remaining three-and-one-half years. Christians elsewhere in the world will flee from the forces of Antichrist (Rev. 12:6 AMP; Matt. 24:16–22).

- **Antichrist will kill** the two witnesses and show their dead bodies to the world for three-and-one-half days. The world will celebrate their deaths (Rev. 11:7–10 AMP).

- **A great earthquake** will strike Jerusalem killing seven thousand people. The two witnesses will be resurrected to life in full view of the world (Rev. 11:11–13 AMP).

- **The sun** will turn black and the moon will turn blood red, stars will fall from the sky as the sky splits and rolls up like a scroll. Mankind will hide in fear as the seas roar (Matt. 24:29, with Rev. 6:12–14 AMP; Acts 2:19–20 AMP).

- **The sign of Christ** will appear in the clouds and his angels will gather those who are worthy and ready to meet him in the air (Matt. 24:30–31 AMP; Rev. 7:9–17 AMP). Those not raptured will have their faith tried to purify them and make them white before God's wrath comes on the earth (Dan. 11:35 AMP).

Last Half of Tribulation—The Seventh Seal—
"The Hour of Trial"

YEAR FIVE—FIRST FOUR TRUMPET JUDGMENTS

- **First trumpet judgment:** One third of the earth, green grass, and trees will be burned up by hail and fire mixed with blood (Rev. 8:7 AMP).

- **Second trumpet judgment:** A blazing mountain-like object will fall into the sea, causing one-third of the sea to turn to blood and destroying one-third of sea life and ships (Rev. 8:8–9 AMP).

- **Third trumpet judgment:** A huge burning star will fall, poisoning one-third of the rivers and springs, causing many to die (Rev. 8:10–11 AMP).

- **Fourth trumpet judgment:** One-third of the sun, moon, and stars will be darkened causing darkness for one-third of both day and night (Rev. 8:12 AMP).

YEAR SIX—FIFTH AND SIXTH TRUMPET JUDGMENTS

During these six judgments, the false prophet will order those who refuse to worship the image of Antichrist to be put to death and will compel all who wish to buy or sell to be marked with the name or number of Antichrist (Rev. 13:15–17 AMP). Three angels flying in mid-heaven will preach the gospel to every nation, warning mankind not to take the mark of the beast and to refuse to worship his image or they will partake of God's wrath (Rev. 14:6–11 AMP).

- **Fifth trumpet judgment:** Smoke from the bottomless pit will darken the sun and air, bringing locust-like scorpions to torment mankind (for five months) who do not have the seal (protection) of God on their foreheads. Men will seek death but will not be permitted to die (Rev. 9:1–11 AMP).

- **Sixth trumpet judgment:** Four fallen angels bound in the Euphrates River for this day will be released to lead 200 million cavalry who will kill one-third of mankind with plagues, fire, and brimstone from the mouths of their steeds (Rev. 9:13–21 AMP).

Year Seven—The Last Trumpet—"The Hour of Wrath"

The seventh trumpet will announce God's wrath. Every believer, either killed (Rev. 20:4) or remaining (Rev. 15:2–3 with Dan. 11:35 AMP), who has not taken the mark of the beast or worshipped his image will be delivered from wrath and "changed" at the sound of the last trumpet (Rev. 15:7; 1 Cor. 15–52). Vials (bowls) of wrath will then be poured out on the kingdom of Antichrist as follows:

- **First bowl:** Grievous sores will strike all who have the mark of the beast and upon those who worship his image (Rev. 16:2).

- **Second bowl:** The sea will turn to putrid blood, killing everything in it (Rev. 16:3).

- **Third bowl:** The rivers and fountains will turn to blood (Rev. 16:4).

- **Fourth bowl:** The sun will scorch mankind with fire, causing them to blaspheme God (Rev. 16:8–9).

- **Fifth bowl:** It will be poured on the headquarters of Antichrist, bringing darkness, sores, and great pain, and causing them to blaspheme God (Rev. 16:10–13).

- **Sixth bowl:** It will be poured on the Euphrates River, drying it up so evil spirits go forth gathering the kings of the earth to Armageddon to battle the Lord (Rev. 16:12–16).

- **Seventh bowl:** It will be poured out on the air, causing thunder, lightning, and the greatest earthquake the earth has ever known, and causing cities throughout the world to fall, every island to disappear, and every mountain to be leveled. Large hailstones will fall on mankind, causing them to blaspheme God (Rev. 16:17–21).

Day of The Lord—"The End of This Age" (Matt. 19:28, 24:3 Amp)

- **A day like none other:** A day of darkness, neither day nor night, known only to the Lord. The world will be a wilderness, with the armies of Antichrist gathered at Armageddon to battle Christ (Zech. 14:6–7; Rev. 16:16 Amp).

- **The Jewish nation will emerge:** The Jewish people and nation will return to their homeland and the armies of Antichrist will then press toward Jerusalem to destroy them (Zech. 14:2–3 Amp).

- **The King will return:** Jesus will return with his saints and his feet will touch down on the Mount of Olives, causing it to split in half from east to west, creating a "very great valley" reaching to a place called Azal (Zech. 14:4–5 Amp).

- **Annihilation of the armies of Antichrist:** A great valley will offer a route of escape for the Jewish nation and a trap for the armies of Antichrist. The Lord will send a great plague on the invaders, causing them to turn their weapons on one another. The plague will consume their flesh, eyes, and tongues. Blood will fill the valley as high as the horse's bridles (Zech. 14:12–13, Rev. 14:20 Amp).

- **Antichrist and false prophet:** The Antichrist and false prophet will be seized and hurled alive into the fiery lake blazing with fire and brimstone (Rev. 19:20 Amp).

- **Satan:** An angel from heaven will overpower Satan and hurl him into the abyss (bottomless pit) where he will be bound for a thousand years. This present age will come to an end (Rev. 20:2–3 Amp).

Beyond Tribulation—Restoration and a New Age

The Thousand Year Reign of Christ on Earth

- **The earth restored:** Restoration will begin with clear, pure, holy water flowing from beneath the altar of the temple in Jerusalem, half flowing toward the Mediterranean Sea and half toward the Dead Sea (Ezek. 47:1–2 AMP; Acts 3:21 AMP).

- **Life is renewed:** Water from beneath the altar will form a river, bringing life to everything it touches. Trees will grow on each side, bearing fruit for food and leaves for healing. Wilderness areas will spring to life and the environment will be new and clean (Ezek. 47:3–12 AMP; Isa. 41:18–20).

- **The promised land:** Israel will be called "Beulah" (married) and its people will be called "Hephzibah" (My Delight). Everyone will know Jerusalem as "The Lord is There" (Isa. 62:4 AMP; Ezek. 48:35 AMP).

- **Law and order:** The saints will judge nations and nations will flow to Beulah Land for festive occasions and to honor the King of Kings. Jerusalem will never be dark or closed day or night (Isa. 60:3, 6, 19–20 AMP; Zech. 8:20–23 AMP).

- **Peace, love, and joy:** Streets and park areas will be full of joy and peace. Old men and women will sit on benches with their canes while boys and girls play in the streets (Zech. 8:4–5). Animals and wildlife will no longer feed on each other but will eat straw and dwell together in peace (Isa. 65:25).

The Last Resurrection, Second Death and the End of the World

- **Satan will be released.** After one thousand years Satan will be released to deceive and gather the nations to battle Christ. They will encompass the saints and Jerusalem about, but will be consumed by fire from God in heaven (Rev. 20:7–9).

- **Satan will be cast into hell.** Satan will be cast into the lake of fire to be tormented day and night eternally (Rev. 20:10).

- **The battle of the ages will end.** Christ will deliver the kingdom to his Father when he has abolished all rule, authority, and power and put all enemies, including death, under his feet (1 Cor. 15:24–28 AMP).

- **The great white throne judgment:** Everyone will stand before the throne of God for judgment (Heb. 9:27; Dan. 7:9–10 AMP). They will be judged by their works, motives, and every idle word spoken (Eccl. 12:14; Matt 12:36–37). Their works will be tried by fire (1 Cor. 3:13–14). Works not consumed will remain. Those who are not found recorded in the Book of Life will be hurled into the lake of fire (Rev. 20:12–15 AMP). This is the second death which has no power over those who were in the first resurrection (Rev. 20:6).

- **The world destroyed:** The present heavens and earth will melt with intense heat, never to be found again (2 Pet. 3:10–12 AMP; Rev. 21:1).

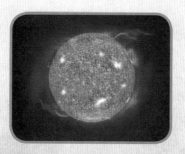

End of Earthly Time   *End of This Present Heaven and Earth*   *End of Earthly Time*

Heaven—Home of the Righteous

A new heaven and a new earth and a New Jerusalem (Isa. 65:17–18, 66:22) will descend from heaven and God will dwell with the saints. The new earth will have no sea, but there will be majestic mountains (Rev 21:1, 10), and there will be no need for the sun or moon (Rev. 21:23).

The Bible offers no further description of the new earth. *(However, the extra-biblical book of I Enoch XXVII–XXXVI tells us that Enoch was shown many animals and birds, clouds and dew, great mountains, streams, valleys, lakes, and many plants and aromatic and colorful trees such as the cinnamon, frankincense, and myrrh in heaven.)*

- **The walls of the city:** The walls of New Jerusalem will be made of solid jasper (Rev 21:18). There will be twelve gates of solid pearl, three on each side, with an angel stationed at each gate, and the names of the twelve tribes of Israel will be written on the gates (Rev. 21:12). The walls will have twelve huge foundations, each of a different precious stone, and each bearing the name of one of the twelve apostles (Rev. 21:14).

- **The eternal city:** The New Jerusalem will be 1,500 miles long, 1,500 miles wide 1,500 miles high. The glory of God and the Lamb will light the city (Rev. 21:23). The city will be pure gold like clear glass (Rev. 21:18) and the main street pure gold (Rev. 21:21 Amp). A river, sparkling like crystal, will run through the middle of the street with the tree of life on both sides of the river (Rev. 22:1–2).

- **The saints:** The Scriptures indicate that the saints will live in mansions (dwellings) (John 14:2), possibly in the land outside the city (Rev. 21:24–26 AMP).

When Christ Reigns

Following the tribulation period, which ends this present age, a new age will begin when Christ will reign with his saints for a thousand years on this present earth. However, the earth will be restored to the way it was when God first formed Adam and Eve and animals and birds.

The similarities of the restored earth and heaven are notable:

- Christ will reign from the present earthly Jerusalem.
- The Father and the Son will reign from New Jerusalem in heaven.

- A river, giving life, will flow from the temple in earthly Jerusalem with trees on its banks, bearing fruit for food and leaves for healing.
- In heaven, a river sparkling like crystal will flow from the throne of God and the lamb, yielding twelve varieties of fruit with a fresh crop every month and leaves for healing.

- The gates of earthly Jerusalem will not be shut day or night.
- The gates of heavenly Jerusalem will never be closed by day and there will be no night there.

- People will continually come to the earthly Jerusalem to worship and serve Jesus.
- In heaven, the saints will come to the throne of God and the Lamb to worship and serve them.

- Righteousness will spring forth on this restored earth and no one will hurt, destroy, or make war any longer.
- In heaven there will no longer exist anything that is accursed, hateful, impure, or offensive.

The following Scriptures relate to this restored earth.

The Restored Earth

RESTORATION
A NEW DAY IS COMING

The ransomed of the LORD shall return, and come to Zion with songs and everlasting joy . . . and sorrow and sighing shall flee away. —Isa. 35:10

The wolf and the lamb shall feed together, and the lion shall eat straw like the bullock. They shall not hurt or destroy in all my holy mountain, saith the LORD.
                                                    —Isa. 65:25

All things have become new

I will open rivers in high places, and fountains in the midst of the valleys…and every thing shall live whither the river cometh.—Isa. 41:18; Ezek. 47:8-9

And by the river upon the banks thereof, on this side and on that side, shall grow all trees…It shall bring forth new fruit according to his months, because their waters they issued out of the sanctuary.—Ezek. 47:12

There shall be no more weeping or sorrow

For in the wilderness shall waters break out, and streams in the desert... The wilderness and the solitary place shall be glad for him; and the desert shall rejoice, and blossom as the rose. —Isa. 35:6,1

The whole earth is at rest, and is quiet: they break forth into singing. —Isa. 14:7

We shall dwell in the house of the Lord forever